BROTHERHOOD OF THE BAG:
THE SUNDAY NIGHT EDITION

BROTHERHOOD OF THE BAG: THE SUNDAY NIGHT EDITION

INCLUDING 100 QUOTES FROM THE MILLIONAIRE WHOLESALER

ROB SHORE

ISBN-13: 0989058026
ISBN-10: 9780989058025
Library of Congress Control Number: 2015912868
CreateSpace Independent Publishing Platform
North Charleston, South Carolina

Acknowledgments

For all the clients, readers, listeners, and audience members, my sincere thanks for the invaluable learning and lessons you provide.

To all the Millionaire Wholesalers we interviewed, thank you for your time and your wisdom.

Table of Contents

About the Word "Brotherhood"

Back in the dark ages of distribution, I remember hearing the phrase "good ole boys club." It was most commonly referenced by women in the wholesaling community who observed that the majority of both frontline wholesalers and their leaders were overwhelmingly male.

Now, some thirty-five years later, this has fortunately changed such that some of the most influential and successful members of the community are female. The title of the book, *Brotherhood of the Bag*, is derived from *Merriam-Webster*'s definition of "brotherhood," which says "the whole body of persons engaged in a business or profession."

Throughout the book the topic of wholesaling is referenced in a gender-neutral fashion, alternating between both male and female references.

Introduction

The Great Recession that started in 2008 could not have come at a worse time. While there is no terrific time for an economic pullback, this one followed closely on the heels of me quitting a lucrative executive-level distribution position in pursuit of a career I'd long dreamed about: entrepreneur.

Specifically, I dreamed of becoming a professional speaker. My goal was to travel the country speaking to advisors and wholesalers about the importance of increasing their MQ—Memorability Quotient®. In hindsight, it was not a plan that was entirely well hatched, but based on my other career successes, I knew I'd figure it out.

That is, until the financial coffers of the companies that I had targeted started to dry up quicker than watering holes in the Sahara Desert.

Needing to get refocused fast, and resolute that I was not ever headed back to corporate America, I recalibrated the business. Instead of incorrectly targeting advisors at all, my attention shifted exclusively to the natural, better place. The place where I had spent the last two decades working, living, and thriving: distribution.

Specifically, my attention shifted to serve only two groups: wholesalers and their leaders.

And rather than simply focusing on speaking, my company needed to include all facets of wholesaler practice management, including education, training, and coaching. It needed to deliver these practice management messages in a host of ways, including online, via podcasts, social media, and emails.

In 2009 I designed a website (www.wholesalermasterminds.com) that served one purpose. It simply offered the Wholesaler Business Plan Template. In exchange for the visitor's name and email address, I gladly provided the template that I'd used to raise billions of dollars.

By the end of 2009, I was sitting on over four hundred email addresses—without a clue of what to do with them.

I knew that the blatant spamming of the community in which I had lived for so long was not the right choice, so I embarked on a process of educating myself about email marketing. I needed to understand how to get the right email messages opened, read, and acted upon.

And so, motivated by what I now acknowledge as the gift of the Great Recession, The *Sunday Night Email* was born.

Since that time, and for the last six-plus years, the *Wholesaler Masterminds® Sunday Night Email* has been landing in recipient's mailboxes every Sunday night at 8:15 p.m. (EST).

This one tool, which now goes out to over twelve thousand wholesalers and leaders around the globe, has been a huge driver of our company's reputation and revenue.

In each *Wholesaler Masterminds® Sunday Night Email*, we strive to offer a 200–250 word bit of infotainment to our readers. Our goal is singular in its purpose: we want to make you a better wholesaler, regardless of your tenure in our great business.

In the following pages, you'll find the collected work of these many Sunday nights.

I hope you enjoy (re-enjoy) them.

The Millionaire Wholesaler

Through our coaching practice at Wholesaler Masterminds®, we know that wholesalers have the strongest desire to understand what the most successful high achievers in our industry are doing to create that success.

During the summer of 2014, we reached out to our community of wholesaling professionals through the following channels:

- *Wholesaler Masterminds® Sunday Night Email* list: more than twelve thousand recipients
- Wholesaler Masterminds® LinkedIn Group: more than forty-three hundred recipients
- Investment Wholesalers of America LinkedIn Group: more than eight thousand members

We requested volunteers who met our qualifying criteria for being interviewed, which was having earnings of $1

1

million in a single year in any year of the last ten years, a current net worth of at least $2.5 million, or both.

For *The Millionaire Wholesaler*™ survey, we conducted more than thirty interviews. Our research attracted seasoned producers, as the majority of those interviewed have fifteen-plus years of wholesaling experience.

The wholesalers, who volunteered on the condition of complete anonymity, spanned the range of products including the following:

- Mutual funds
- Variable annuity
- REITS
- Fixed annuity
- Life insurance
- Managed futures

These phone interviews, which were all transcribed, asked a range of in-depth questions that were standardized across all the interviewees. The queries focused on many concepts that comprise all aspects of wholesaling, including territory process, success strategies, work habits, infrastructure of support systems, personal wealth management, industry-specific challenges, and more.

Specifically, the questions we asked included the following:

- What three things do you attribute your success to?
- What wholesaling habits have you formed that you would recommend to others?
- What do you feel is the one single habit/ritual/action that has contributed to your success?
- There is usually someone that every successful person relies on. In this business we have so many balls in the air; who is that person (spouse, internal, sales manager, etc.)?
- How have you been able to remain relevant?
- Describe your PVP—Peerless Value Proposition®/ what are you best known for in your region?
- What's the greatest danger wholesalers face today?
- What is your net worth?
- Based on your success, what have you done consistently to be able to earn and keep a significant net worth?
- If you had a message to give other wholesalers that would be influential to their success, what would that be?

The findings revealed a wealth of wisdom and advice for maintaining high performance and career longevity in this ultracompetitive marketplace. Again and again, common traits for success (many of which are transferable to any sales role in the distributor) came through loud and clear: drive, perseverance, follow-up process, sticking to your word, and maintaining integrity.

How to Use This Book

In total *Brotherhood of the Bag: The Sunday Night Edition* contains 185 of our most read email messages written over the last six years. Generally speaking, they are presented in chronological order from the oldest to the newest posts. Occasionally we have moved a few stories around to better assist the overall flow of the book.

The one hundred selected *Millionaire Wholesaler™* quotations you find throughout the book are taken directly from the work we did with our *Millionaire Wholesaler* survey participants. More quotes can be found via search at Twitter using the hashtag #themillionairewholesaler.

We hope you'll find lessons, reminders, and insights worthy of underlining, highlighting, and dog-earring multiple pages and passages as you work your way through the book.

The Sunday Night Emails

Wholesalers and High Concepts

Quick.

Describe the essence of what you do for advisors in a short sentence.

Make it both brief and provocative.

Will it pique the prospect's imagination and promise that good things are going to happen out of an otherwise-ordinary wholesaler encounter?

In the late 1960s, two TV executives needed a way to get you and me, after reading *TV Guide*, to choose their shows over all other listings.

They came up with what is now known in Hollywood as the "high concept."

Without the high concept, your script won't get read, your project won't get funded, and your show won't be watched.

To separate yourself from the masses in our business, you need a well-polished high concept (a.k.a. PVP—Peerless Value Proposition®).

It will help to ensure that your message will be heard and your brand will be understood.

What's your PVP?

The Seamy Underbelly of Wholesaling

True confession time.

You may know Dr. Pavlov and his dogs.

In the early 1900s, he discovered that the dogs in his lab were conditioned to salivate even before the food was shown—they started to drool as soon as he entered the room.

And, sadly, so it was for me as a new wholesaler.

Mistakenly thinking that the allure of my Visa card was the righteous path to attracting top producers.

When, in reality, all I attracted using that tactic was top-flight slimeballs.

The cycle of "I'll do for you, and only then will you produce for me" was not only soul-sucking; it was also tentative.

If another wholesaler had a bigger credit line and far fewer scruples, then the producers simply moved on.

My relationship with these asshat advisors was not based on reciprocal exchange of ideas and outcomes—it was based on one part insecurity and two parts greed.

Insecurity that stemmed from my early lack of confidence in my innate wholesaling skills, combined with the greed that surrounds us in commissioned sales.

You and I both know that this less savory side of the business exists.

But the greatest of the great wholesalers earn their wild success while managing to steer clear of the seamy underbelly of our world.

———

**"Do things by the rules—
be compliance aware."**
—The Millionaire Wholesaler

Three Questions to Ask Yourself

To date, Wholesaler Masterminds® has spent over forty-five hundred hours coaching and training wholesalers and their leaders.

We like to ask the following three questions from time to time:

1. As a wholesaler, what one trait or characteristic are you most proud to display to clients and prospects?

2. What one flaw do you hope they will never see?

3. What is the one change that you could make to your brand, process, presentations, relationships, or prospecting and organizational skills that would catapult you to the next level of desired success?

Think about how would you answer them—and, more importantly, what have you done to exploit, address, or remedy each of these?

Nobody Works Past Five O'clock

One Monday the heater in our spa went on the blink.

It seemed that the flame on the gas-fed unit was not firing.

So I called the pool guy who services it, and he gladly informed me that he had a "heater guy" whom he'd get on the case right away.

Four days passed, so I called him again on Thursday afternoon at 4:58 p.m.

Me: Did you get hold of the heater guy, and when is he coming to fix it?

Pool Guy: My day was slammed, and I completely forgot to call him...(brief pause)...and it's five o'clock. Nobody works past five, so I'll call him in the morning.

Really?

––––––

**"Work hard and don't be afraid
to do those extra meetings."**
–The Millionaire Wholesaler

Exact Change Required

Some years ago, I was riding with a brand-new wholesaler whom I hired, and we were approaching a busy tollbooth on the I-294.

He pulled up to the Exact Change coin bin and frantically searched for any money.

Then he looked at me with sheer terror in his eyes as the docile citizens of Chicago, stacking up behind us, began to lose their patience.

Panicked, he was frozen in place at the toll plaza.

I got out and begged the car behind us to take one dollar in return for two quarters.

Be ready for everything and overlook nothing when your manager is coming for a ride-a-long.

I Might Need an Intervention

One recent evening, I was sitting on the couch relaxing, which for me generally means TV on and an electronic device extending from the tip of my fingers.

In an attempt to look at a friend's QR code that I had seen on Facebook with my iPad, I grabbed my iPhone to actually shoot the image with a QR-reader application.

You following me?

Then it was time to write to you, so I grabbed my laptop to churn this out.

And in that moment, I looked down and saw my iPhone, iPad, and laptop all within inches of where I was seated.

And I thought, "Rob, you need an intervention!"

If we're not careful, that technological umbilical cord will strangle us.

Confessions of a Hotel Snob

Back in the early 2000s, I was down in Macon, Georgia, riding with a wholesaler.

We put in a full day of five solid appointments and then a dinner, and it was time to find the hotel for the night.

And that's when it got ugly.

My experience via these six signs confirmed, yet again, that I am a bona fide hotel snob.

1. The registration window was just off of the parking lot.

2. The doors to the rooms all faced outward, toward the same parking lot.

3. The front-desk clerk had an economy of teeth.

4. The room was prepaid before the key was released to the guest.

5. The pillows on the bed were more roundish—and made of foam.

6. The bed squeaked at the slightest move.

Safe travels!

Time to Do My Nails

I've admitted it before, and I'll admit it again: I tend to be a workaholic.

And no, it's not something I'm proud of.

One time I had a key account manager come out to my region from New York. Before her arrival, I shared with her a list of local target firms I was trying to get selling agreements with—assuming she would reach out to them during her visit.

After connecting with her by phone the morning she landed in Los Angeles, we agreed that she would meet me at a seminar where I was speaking later that night.

Upon arriving at the seminar, I excitedly asked how her visits with our clients and my target firms went.

She matter-of-factly and somewhat indignantly replied, "Huh? I got a manicure!"

Lesson #1: She was not a workaholic.

Lesson #2: Assume nothing.

———

"Hard work and good relationships are attributes of being successful."
—*The Millionaire Wholesaler*

My Girl Whoopi

Are you familiar with 30 Rockefeller Plaza in New York City?

You may know that high atop 30 Rock once stood the Rainbow Room, which used to be open for dining and made a great place to entertain reps.

One late Saturday night, after a due-diligence dinner in the mid-1990s, I exited the building with an advisor named Alice on my arm (she was, how shall we say, drunk).

Alice was African American, and she wore her hair in long dreadlocks.

If you and I have not met, know that I am Caucasian, tall, and thin.

As we made our way through the revolving door to the street, a small crowd started to descend on us with pens and photos in hand.

They were immediately crushed when they realized that I was not the host of *Saturday Night Live* that week (Ted Danson), and Alice was not his then-fling Whoopi Goldberg!

Fame.

So Fleeting.

Bad Decisions in Bozeman

My first wholesaling territory covered eight Western states.

One of them was Montana.

One night in Bozeman, I assumed that a great way to spend the evening was to find a game of poker at a local bar.

Makes sense, right?

A California kid looking for a poker game in a blue-collar cowboy town.

In the back room of a seedy watering hole, I found a game, and, in what any of my friends will tell you is a most un-likely occurrence, I won big.

And then I had to gauge how I would extricate myself from the game without getting my ass kicked.

It was then that I knew that this great profession was going to provide the most amazing experiences.

Ready for the Fall Campaign?

Hope you had a great Labor Day.

And now the year-end push begins.

Last week I got this message in the comments of one of my blog posts:

Rob,
Been a very long time. See that you are still doing what you do best. Thought about you a lot over the years. You made an everlasting impression on me, and I'm sure it's same with your coaching and training today.

Why do I share this with you?

Because it came from an advisor that I called on as a wholesaler more than twelve years ago and had not spoken to since.

It reminds me that *you* make a meaningful impact on people every single day—and you may not ever find out.

So keep on doing what you do best, making big impacts, and you'll finish the year with a flourish.

Top Producers Gone Wild

Back in the days when mutual fund companies were allowed to do swanky due-diligence trips, I invited a few of my top dogs to New York City.

The first event of the trip was always the welcome reception at the Marriott World Trade Center.

It was at that event that I knew Dave was going to be a handful.

You see Dave was the advisor who got louder the more he drank.

And he really liked to drink.

On Saturday I escorted folks uptown to watch college football, and naturally beers and assorted Bloody Marys ensued.

By late afternoon Dave was louder and more belligerent than I ever dreamed possible and was mouthing off to random strangers on the street.

I found myself torn between leaving his drunken butt wandering the mean streets and feeling responsible for making sure he didn't get the crap beat out of him.

What do you do when top producers go wild?

———

"Don't forget who brought you to the dance. Take care of your best producers."
—*The Millionaire Wholesaler*

Pool Man Jumped the Shark, So I Fired Him

Like many Southern Californians, I have water in my back-yard—an in-ground spa.

It's small enough to care for myself yet large enough that I don't want to.

Enter: Terry, the Pool Man.

During his pitch to get the job, Pool Man outlined all of the services he would perform on each visit.

He prided himself on his ability to do the job more knowledgeably, consistently, and reliably than his competition.

For the first year, his weekly service was quite good.

And then things changed.

He started to skip weeks—and charge me for them.

Pool Man was hired to check chemicals, empty filter baskets, sweep, and vacuum.

Over time, one or more of these items was not performed with each visit as promised.

Pool Man's reliability decreased, and his excuses increased.

Finally, after three weeks of no show, no email, no call, and no nothing, Pool Man was fired.

He started taking my business and loyalty for granted.

A promise of consistency translated over time into haphazardness.

A promise of reliability deteriorated into unpredictability.

Pool Man had jumped the shark.

He was now in decline.

What about your business?

As you take a step back and critically evaluate yourself, your region, your division, and/or your team, are you living up to the original commitments made to prospects, now clients?

———

"Always do what you say you are going to do."
—*The Millionaire Wholesaler*

Why Wholesaling Is like Roofing Tiles, Only Different

Recently we had our house tented for termites—an event that I wish on no one that you know and certainly not on you.

If you are not familiar (can we trade places?), this is where many five-foot-tall men show up and swarm your roof, placing huge tarps that "wrap" the whole house in a somewhat airtight seal so that the gas, which will surely kill any and all things it comes in contact with, will stay in the wrapper.

Got the picture?

Anyway, as you might imagine: people walking on your roof = cracked roof tiles.

In my search for replacement tiles (Mission style, both field and edge, if you must know), I went to retailer #1 who insisted that the field tile was no longer made and that I would need to go to another place that reclaims tiles from old homes.

So I went.

And the salesman there pulled out the sales brochure and asked me which of eight color styles I'd like to purchase—new.

Are you following me?

Lesson: Never insist that something is irrefutably one way if you even have the slightest thought that you might be wrong.

In this situation the salesman at retailer #1 was dead wrong, which proved to me that he—and perhaps by extension his company—didn't know their products.

Result?

I can't shop there in the future (heaven forbid) because I don't trust their expertise.

Laila Wanted Me Fired

When I first started wholesaling, I assumed a territory that had been covered by Gail.

Gail had been with the firm for a long, long time and was good at what she did—in fact, she was a top producer.

She wasn't exactly thrilled that the bank channel had been lifted out from her region and given to me.

Sadly, her lack of enthusiasm for my arrival on her scene was made clear to all, including our clients.

Laila was the manager of a small program that did a fair amount of the firm's business before I arrived.

During my first visit with Laila, I must have said or done something that set her off because she didn't hesitate to call my boss and complain.

Yet, the biggest complaint she had was that I wasn't Gail.

In my next meeting with her, I brought up her complaint and the fact that, though I will never be (nor wished to be) Gail, she should expect great things from our relationship and that I was troubled she thought it appropriate to go to my boss.

And do you know what happened next?

She apologized.

And she admitted that she had no basis, other than Gail leaving, for her complaint.

And that she would like to wipe the slate clean and start fresh.

And so we did.

And every year for seven years, all the folks in her office, including her, were $1-million producers.

The right amount of candor, diplomatically dispensed, can often yield unexpectedly terrific results.

Simple, Not Easy

DeeAnne was a wholesaler in Northern California.

On a ride-a-long with her, we stopped off at the office of Fred, who was the eleven-hundred-pound producer at his broker/dealer.

DeeAnne explained to me that Fred only gave her ten minutes, so she was closing for another, longer appointment.

Frankly I couldn't tell if the meeting was successful—but who can tell in ten minutes?

Later that week Fred called DeeAnne for help on a large ticket.

She called back promptly.

Fred dropped a $600,000 ticket.

Later, DeeAnne learned from Fred that on that day he called five wholesalers for help—one right after another.

Two have still yet to return his call—and this was more than eight years ago.

Two thought that twenty-four hours were good enough response time.

One—that would be DeeAnne—jumped on the call.

You see, operating with a high degree of urgency is simple but not easy.

If urgency was important to the eleven-hundred-pound gorilla Fred eight years ago, how much more important is it today in a world of hyperconnected advisors?

I'm No Spring Chicken

Not quite over the hill mind you but old enough to be able to reflect on things that you may not have seen, heard, or thought about.

Take bank interest rates…stay with me here.

Before 1983 every bank had the same rate on the same type of account.

In a world where everyone was paying 4.5 percent for bank deposits, how did any one institution stand out from the pack and avoid this Sea of Sameness?

To one bank it was the "save by mail" service. To another it was the allure of stashing your money in California.

As for me, I want the three-piece silver-plated salad set.

So what does this have to do with wholesaling today?

Everything!

Precious few wholesalers have anything truly unique, product-wise, in their bag.

That means you need to strengthen your MQ—Memorability Quotient®—the characteristics, attributes, talents, or processes that allow you to break out of the 4.5 percent pack.

———

"The only way you're going to succeed long term is to have your own brand."
—The Millionaire Wholesaler

My Infraction of Ignorance

Freedom.

What wholesaler doesn't enjoy it?

So what could be better than hitting the open road on that rare chance you have to drive an open highway?

My first trip to the Big Sky state included uncontrollable anticipation for the experience of having no speed limit on a major interstate.

After validating this notion with my Montana reps, I learned two things:

1. No speed limit is a myth, but speeding was mostly ignored.

2. If pulled over, the fine for speeding was five dollars— *payable to the officer who pulled you over.*

So I set out for the two-plus-hour drive from Billings to Bozeman.

At ninety to one hundred miles per hour.

In the oncoming lane, a Montana Highway Patrol cruiser was approaching.

He immediately dipped into the median and shot up on my side of the highway, lights signaling for me to pull over.

As he checked my license and registration, observed my dress (suit and tie), and smirked at my California driver's license (he did), I uttered the words that I will forever regret.

"Well, this will only be a five-dollar ticket, right?"

It was then that he placed me in the back of the police cruiser while explaining that it was up to him to determine if a fine or reckless driving were more appropriate infractions.

After running my license through the law-enforcement databases and determining that the biggest threat I posed was appearing woefully overdressed in a land of jeans and cowboy hats, he let me go.

After I paid him the five-dollar fine—in cash.

Brief and Occasional Train Noise

Shortcomings.

We all have them.

And sometimes we choose, unwisely, to overlook them in others.

Recently The Mrs. and I took a journey up to the Pacific Northwest and booked a hotel that had great reviews, was right on the water, and had a spa.

And it was right on the train tracks.

Prior to booking the trip, the following exchange took place with my wife.

Me: "Looks like the nicest place in town for us to stay is right on the train tracks."

Wife: "That's OK with me. I like trains—you know how they put me to sleep."

Upon check-in there was a small plaque tucked over to the right side of the registration desk that said, "Brief and Occasional Train Noise."

I said to the front desk clerk, "Wow, you are really close to the tracks!"

To which she replied, "No problem; we have ear plugs in the room."

Uh-oh.

At 3:00 a.m., a freight train rolled through.

Judging by its size, I am fairly certain that the train had most of what the city of Vancouver, British Columbia, needed for the next month contained in its endless stream of cars.

After that train, this is the exchange that took place.

Me: "You awake?"

Wife: "I guess trains only put me to sleep when I'm riding on them…"

And so it continued. For all four days we were there.

These are the lessons I learned:

1. Other good components of the business (spa, décor, view) can't make up for fundamental flaws.

2. You can't put lipstick on a pig. The staff at the hotel can't downplay the noise created by five trains per night.

3. Customers might try you once (as we did), but those fundamental flaws will damage your chance for a loyal, lasting tribe of followers and raving fans.

Ten Rules of Wholesaling

The wisdom of our elders.

I was speaking at the CFDD Conference in Chicago and was introduced to a long-tenured wholesaler.

He's been around so long that telephones with a dial (versus crank) had just come into vogue when he started his career!

As we spoke over an adult beverage, he told me he had Ten Rules of Wholesaling.

I insisted that he share them with me, so I could share them with you.

Here they are:

1. Don't wholesale during family time (on vacation, etc.).

2. Don't spend any time dissing the competition.

3. Don't eat alone (makes you look like a loser).

4. Don't swear—no matter how much you want to. No f-bombs.

5. Send your expense account weekly. Absolutely no padding.

6. Keep your car clean.

7. Never tell another advisor what you are working on.

8. Be discrete and moderate at all company sales meetings.

9. Treat your internal with respect, kindness, and professionalism.

10. Never tell anyone how much you earn. Never. Ever.

Go Lie Down

Have you ever built a house or done a major remodel?

If yes, then you know the builder "walk-through."

If not, stay with me anyway.

In a newly built home, this is where you are handed a tick sheet and asked to go through the house and note any of the issues that the builder needs to resolve.

One of my coworkers suggested lying face up on the floor in the middle of each room.

He said that when you lie on the floor, you'll observe things from that perspective that you would otherwise miss from a conventional viewpoint.

Go ahead. Try it.

Never noticed that nail pop in the drywall, did you?

Taking on this different angle sharpens your powers of observation.

How keen are your wholesaling powers of observation?

One time I was calling on the head of product for a gigantic broker/dealer that our firm needed to secure. The meeting took place in the product manager's office, and I had one of my wholesalers with me.

When we left the meeting, he started rattling off all of the things that he had observed in her office.

The folks in her pictures.

The books on her shelves.

The knickknacks on her credenza.

We then discussed ways to forge a relationship with her based on what we had seen.

Do you need to sharpen your powers of observation?

Just One Great Sales Idea

You know Ben, right?

Benjamin Franklin, that is.

In 1758 he published a book called *The Way to Wealth*, written as a preface to *Poor Richard's Almanack*.

In only thirty pages, he delivers all of the goodness you'd expect from a guy who gets his picture on the one-hun-dred-dollar bill.

In fact, this book is where two of Ben's all-time greatest hits come from:

"Early to bed and early to rise makes a man healthy, wealthy, and wise."

"There are no gains without pains."

And, if you read the book carefully, you'll find dozens more.

Idea: What if you bought copies for your top twenty-five producers, inscribed the inside cover with a personal mes-sage, and shot it out to them in the mail?

Think your MQ—Memorability Quotient®—will go up?

Did Ben fly a kite?

How to Butcher a Prospect

My dad is eighty-three.

At this point in his life, he is making sure that his financial house is in order, both for his future and for the future of his family.

And he needs a financial advisor to assist him.

While I am licensed, frankly I am not capable, it would be like practicing medicine on your family member.

I was referred to an advisor near my dad's home, and I called.

Me: "May I speak to Peter, please?"

Receptionist: "He's away from his desk. Can he call you right back?"

Peter returned the call…four days later.

In the meantime, I got ticked off because where I come from "away from his desk" doesn't translate into calling back four days later.

It turns out that Peter was not away from his desk—he was on personal time off.

And so began an unnecessarily rocky start to what might be a great prospect for the advisor.

Making sure your message is delivered in the right manner; seems so simple, doesn't it?

Too bad it's just not that easy.

———

"Be honest with yourself and your prospects you are talking to."
—*The Millionaire Wholesaler*

Catsup or Ketchup—It's Still Heinz

On my way back from the gym last week, I was listening to an interview on National Public Radio.

The interviewee, a chef, was answering questions about what's tastier/easier—a homemade product or store-bought products.

For example, bacon = store bought (no argument here).

When the chef was asked about ketchup, she said, "If it doesn't taste like Heinz, it doesn't taste like ketchup."

She explained that no matter how terrific the homemade version was, the baseline against which it will be measured is Heinz.

So I wondered how many wholesalers are content to be near imitations of greatness and how many are setting the standard?

Are you Hunt's or Del Monte, constantly chasing from behind, or are you the leader in your market—that others fear and wish to emulate?

What if this is the year you decided to establish your dominance?

What if you decided that this is going to be your Career Year?

The Croissant

There it sat in the display case in all of its golden, glistening, light, flaky goodness.

The light from the pristinely clean glass was illuminating my craving, making it irresistible.

While the angel on one shoulder was saying, "Don't do it," the devil in me was screaming, "Just eat it!"

So I caved and ordered the croissant.

As I tore off a piece, I anticipated the melt-in-your-mouth flavor.

And as I bit down, I almost chipped a tooth.

Yep, stale.

Hard. As. A. Rock.

It's kind of like wholesaling.

Just because you wear a $2,000 suit, carry a Tumi bag, and look great on the outside doesn't mean that your skills— after many years in the field—haven't become stale.

I remember speaking to a crazy successful wholesaler (a Millionaire Wholesaler) who was exploring coaching because he was concerned about that very fact.

He was looking to have a Career Year.

Are you?

————

"You've got to stay current."
—*The Millionaire Wholesaler*

Sometimes I'm Not Too Bright

When I covered Southern California, being stuck in traffic was a regular occurrence.

And like any time I was in the car, I was on the phone.

With advisors, COIs, prospects, and, of course, my internal wholesaler.

One particular internal and I had a great, albeit sometimes cantankerous, relationship, and we raised a boat load of money.

One day I was giving him direction on a task that needed to be completed for the region.

He saw the outcome differently than I did.

We began to argue like a salty old married couple.

And then I threw out this: "Just f*@%ing do it—it's MY territory!"

Oh boy, talk about the wrong thing to say.

We spent the next ten minutes arguing about who owned the territory.

What a dummy I was.

If he cared enough to fight about who owned the territory, wasn't that a good thing?

———

"My internal is the most integral part of my business."

—*The Millionaire Wholesaler*

Stiletto Heels and Power Washers

We all have our "thing."

One is my frustration dealing with minimum-required people (MRP).

Another is my disdain for having my car serviced.

I guess it's the fact that I have no idea what's really wrong with the car and all the control is in the hands of the servicer.

That, and it's usually a horrible customer-service experience.

Recently, I went to the dealer to have my 2006 Honda Ridgeline pickup (don't judge) serviced.

The service writer, a petite young woman (who was fashionably dressed and in stiletto heels), wrote me up and said the car would be ready at 8:30 a.m.

As the only thing it required was an oil change and one of their handy 362-Point Inspections, I decided to wait for the car to be done.

At 8:29 a.m. I looked over at the car-wash bay—as that's the final step before giving me my car back—and noticed that, since all the other workers were busy, she was washing my truck.

With a power washer.

In her stiletto heels.

My car was handed back to me at 8:30 a.m. as promised.

Clearly she's not an MRP.

One Wholesaler Over the Cuckoo's Nest

One of my favorite movies of all time (after *Airplane!*) is *One Flew Over the Cuckoo's Nest*.

In that 1972 classic set in a mental ward, Jack Nicholson, in the role of McMurphy, says, "Who's the head bull-goose loony around here?"

And some wholesalers are bull-goose loony—if not insane.

You are familiar with the definition of insanity, aren't you?

It's doing the same thing over and over yet expecting a different result.

Rep meeting—product dump—internal follow-up—expect the advisor's business.

Rep meeting—product dump—internal follow-up—expect the advisor's business.

Lather.

Rinse.

Repeat.

Bull-goose loony wholesaler thinks, "Where's the money, I did what I was supposed to do."

Sadly this happens countless times every day to endless numbers of wholesalers.

That's why we like a Systematized Follow-up Process.

The process is preprogrammed so that you know exactly what's supposed to happen, and when, for each segment/stage of your business.

Through this process you can stay in front of advisors (including using your PVP—Peerless Value Proposition®) to earn the business you richly deserve.

———

"Have a definable, repeatable, disciplined process."

—*The Millionaire Wholesaler*

Yes, I Do Windows Too

The things we do to bring in a buck.

An advisor in central California asked me if I would do a seminar for his credit union customers.

As he was a top producer, of course the answer was yes.

After a four-hour drive to Lompoc (yes, it's as out of the way as it sounds), I arrived at the branch.

The first order of business was to set up the room.

Which for most seminars is fairly standard stuff.

Unless it entails moving all of the regular branch-lobby furniture out of the lobby and replacing it with one hundred folding chairs.

Did I mention the part about how the two of us were the only ones doing the setup?

Or the fact that it was in the middle of a summer heat wave?

By the time the seminar attendees arrived, I was bathed in sweat.

And twenty minutes into the presentation, the bulb on his projector burned out—and he didn't have a replacement.

Sometimes it's just too glamorous a job—you know?

Small World, Big Memories

There I sat at the Admirals Club DFW after a wholesaler national sales-meeting presentation.

The bartender was explaining to me the cruel joke he plays on people who annoy him.

He starts singing one of those awful songs that sticks in your head like bubble gum to the bottom of your Allen Edmonds/Jimmy Choos.

Songs such as "It's a Small World."

Ironically when I got home, I found an email from a wholesaler who knows the advisor who I wrote about two weeks ago in "Yes, I Do Windows Too."

The advisor writes:

"Glad the event left as big an impression on Rob as it did on me.

He actually offered to rent a hotel next time at his expense—he was in hell; physical labor wasn't his thing!

We went to a local bar afterward, and the bartender screwed up his drink order three times in a row! It was just amazing. I still laugh about that night myself."

It's a small world indeed.

Not Quite Happy Hour Just Yet

"When it's time to go home, make one more call."

That's the advice a sales manager gave me a long time ago.

And it's still true today.

One more appointment per day.

What would happen if you did just one more appointment per day?

Or four more appointments more per week (if you take an office day).

That's sixteen more appointments per month.

Which equals 192 more appointments per year.

And that, my friends, is how you're creating your next Career Year.

———

"Have the work ethic to get the appointments on your calendar."
—The Millionaire Wholesaler

You Gotta Get Your Teeth Kicked In

At OppenheimerFunds, I spent a ton of time training future bank-platform reps to sell mutual funds for CalFed Bank (may they rest in peace).

Each month, the Mutual Funds One class would begin with participant introductions.

From the wide eyes and hesitant voices, I could tell that these new Account Representatives were not quite ready to embark on the company mandate—selling nondeposit products to bank clients.

By day three, after filling their brains with an inordinate amount of information, but before turning them loose on the investing public, I asked them about their level of confidence.

Most replied that they were worried—worried about sounding or looking bad.

I reminded them that everyone starting out must "get their teeth kicked in."

They needed to risk looking/sounding less than perfect (or even downright foolish) the first few times they made a presentation to have any hope of becoming a great investment sales professional.

And changing the way you wholesale is no different.

———

"Embrace change and not be afraid of it."
—*The Millionaire Wholesaler*

Congratulations, Your Clients Now Own You

It was 5:30 p.m., and I was driving the 405 south through Orange County.

The phone rang, and it was one of my advisors.

Not just any advisor but my largest.

He called to ask for money for a marketing campaign that would be "featuring" my fund family.

The amount he requested was really out of bounds for my budget.

Using my best negotiating *attempt*, I threw a counter offer on the table.

And he played the following card:

"Why are we negotiating if I am your largest client?"

Rewind the clock ninety days, and you will find me at dinner with this client.

Somewhere between the before-dinner cocktails and the main course, I made the pivotal mistake that offered me a great lesson: I told him, by number, exactly where he ranked in sales in my territory.

And on that fateful day, the balance of power shifted.

Here is my ~~suggestion for~~ gift to you: never, under any circumstances, tell your clients *exactly* where they rank in sales.

Ranges such as, "You're one of my twenty best producers," sure.

Exact ranking?

Never.

And I Walked to School Uphill, Both Ways

It must have been 1967 or so.

My parents had just sunk a bunch of money into the full set of *Encyclopedia Britannica*—from *A* to *Z*, plus the accompanying dictionaries.

For years those books were the de facto way to do any and every form of investigative research without having to walk to the local library.

Now, 235 years later, *Encyclopedia Britannica* in its printed form is no more.

The print version was rendered unnecessary in a digital world.

It's now an extinct relic of an era gone by.

And if wholesalers are not careful, they could end up in the same boneyard as yesterday's printed media.

———

"Being a student of your industry really helps you remain relevant."
—The Millionaire Wholesaler

Wholesaling Chicken or Wholesaling Egg?

I received a question via email that gave me pause for thought. I decided to put it into one of my Sunday Night Emails and ask for reader input.

And input I got!

Here's the question I received:

I would be interested to hear your thoughts on the following question that I was recently asked in an interview, "Which came first: the relationship or the sale?"

The question came from a sales manager who believes relationships are good, but they don't get you the sale.

Really?

My reply was:

Short answer—relationship.

Period.

If the advisor doesn't connect with you on some level (relationship), there will be no sale.

————

"Success is about building relationships."

—The Millionaire Wholesaler

They Made the Cable Company Look Good

Maybe I should still be a renter.

Reason being, when stuff breaks you call the landlord.

The repair de jour is now the U-Line wine fridge and the Thermadore oven—in order of priority!

The repair service I called gave me a three-hour window (bad sign), and at the two-hour and fifty-five-minute mark, I called to ask where they were.

"We'll be there within thirty minutes," was the reply.

To which I said, "If I wanted to be made to feel like my business didn't matter, I would have scheduled the cable company!"

Next time when you know you are running late for an appointment, for heaven's sake proactively call—don't just show up late, even if it's only five minutes.

Sound basic?

Yes.

Does everyone do it?

Absolutely not.

Simple, not easy, way to increase your MQ—Memorability Quotient®?

No doubt.

———

"Be on time to your meeting."
—The Millionaire Wholesaler

The Lowest-Paying White-Collar Job

The noble bank teller.

In the late 1970s, that's how I started my journey in financial services.

Banks were just starting to interject sales into the retail-bank formula.

So we were taught to cross-sell and offered statistics about how the stickiness of a client relationship was directly correlated to the number of services the client had.

Checking only = high risk to leave.

Checking + mortgage loan + auto loan + CD = high likelihood to stay.

And so it is with wholesaling.

Product-spewing wholesaler equals an advisor with a high likelihood to leave you when your product falls out of favor.

Meaningful to the advisor relationship on multiple levels through your PVP—Peerless Value Proposition® (practice management, case/portfolio design, staff training, etc.)—equals an advisor with a high likelihood to weather performance or pricing speed bumps.

———

"You've got to be more than the product."

—The Millionaire Wholesaler

If It Walks Like a Duck

Travel is glamorous.

Especially in taxis found in any metropolitan city.

In fact, I'd like to have a word with the guy who decided that a Toyota Prius can be converted into a cab.

Since I stand six feet two, it's more like a form of urban torture than transportation.

This week I had the good fortune to travel to Toronto to speak to a group of wholesalers.

Upon exiting the airport, I saw two lines—one for taxis and one for limos.

The oddity was that both lines had the exact same cars—black Lincoln Town Cars.

I jumped into a taxi.

As we drove off, I asked the driver what the difference was between the "limo" in front of us and his cab.

"Service and price, sir," was his reply. "We have better service, and our prices are lower."

As I looked around the spotless interior of the car, I saw a holder for the company's business cards.

Grabbing a card for the return trip back to the airport, I noticed one other piece of marketing ingenuity.

The card offered "Free Wake-Ups."

Never mind that in the age of the smartphone, you don't need one—the fact that they offer the service gives them extra points.

How ingenious is your MQ—Memorability Quotient®?

———

"Differences sell, similarities don't."
—The Millionaire Wholesaler

Sympathy Is a Wasted Emotion

"Sympathy is a wasted emotion."

Those were the words that I heard from a teacher of psychology many years ago.

What he expressed was that rather than feeling the same emotion as, in our case, a financial advisor, you'd be better served to practice empathy.

Formally the difference is as follows:

> sym-pa-thy: feelings of pity and sorrow for someone else's misfortune

> em-pa-thy: the ability to understand and share the feelings of another

This memory came alive for me this week while speaking at the Investment Management Consultants Association (IMCA) meeting in Washington, DC. I entered into a discussion with a high-end advisor.

When I asked him his general opinion about wholesalers, his reply was—how shall we say—tepid.

One statement in particular that he made resonated.

He said, "Wholesalers need to remember that they are three emotions removed—they don't have to deal with the end client."

What I heard him saying is that not enough wholesalers demonstrate the qualities that suggest that they truly care about the advisor's business—in this case, listening to understand with empathy.

Do you listen simply to find the opening in the verbal joust, only so you can jam the next product idea on the advisor?

Or do you listen with empathy—a skill set only great wholesalers possess?

Defending the Honor of Wholesaling

Do you remember Dudley Do-Right?

A cartoon character from the 1960s, he was the dim-witted, cheerful, and conscientious Canadian Mountie who fell hopelessly for his love interest Nell.

In episode after episode, Dudley was seen defending Nell from the evil Snidely Whiplash.

What's this got to do with wholesaling, you ask?

Everything.

Last week I wrote to you about the advisor at the IMCA conference who spoke unkindly about wholesalers in general.

A wholesaler reader of The Sunday Night Email let me know that that ticked him off.

He suggested that we as a community should be more forceful in our defense of the honor of wholesaling and less willing to accept any "wholesaler bashing."

He offered that he is always prepared to display all of the quality attributes of great wholesalers—if only the advisor would do him the courtesy of returning a phone call, answering an email, or keeping an appointment.

And you know what? He's right.

For the segment of advisors who insist on being Snidely Whiplash and denigrating the craft that so many do so well, we should employ our best Dudley Do-Right and defend the honor of the craft.

Everywhere Is Walking Distance If You Have the Time

"Everywhere is walking *distance if you have the time."*
– Steven Wright

It's all about perspective, isn't it?

Sometimes we need someone with a completely different view of the world to reframe our thoughts.

One time my assistant got a call from one of our wholesalers who had received a call from our corporate credit-card company, telling her that her stolen credit card had been found.

On a dead body!

Without blinking an eye, the assistant commented, "That's good; at least the card hasn't been used yet."

Next time you are staring down into the vortex of wholesaling insanity, go seek out someone with an alternative thought process to rearrange your perspective.

––––––

"Have the discipline to constantly revamp your system."
—The Millionaire Wholesaler

Are You a First-Call Wholesaler?

What's a first-call wholesaler, you ask?

Here's a related example I heard about from an executive at a credit union.

She told me about a service concept called PlusOne and the flagship story that exemplifies it.

They call it the "Snapple Factor."

It seems that a member called into a credit-union call center for some advice.

Was she calling about her CD choices?

No.

Did she need guidance about whether she could refinance her mortgage loan?

No.

She was calling to get help about what size Snapple would give her the best value for her money.

Apparently she was at the grocery store and wanted to make the right, savvy buying decision.

The call-center rep unflinchingly gave her the best answer that was possible, and the member continued shopping—knowing that her credit union had come to her aid...again.

First-call wholesalers are like that.

They instill such a great sense of trust and confidence in the advisor that the advisor feels completely comfortable using the wholesaler for the broadest range of information, as a sounding board or even as a confidant.

Are you a first-call wholesaler?

Eight Ounces of Water Worth $5,000?

Vacation season is upon us.

And The Mrs. and I are just back from the wine country, where we tend to gravitate to—a lot.

On one of our trips some five years ago, we drove to a then-newer resort tucked up in the north end of Napa Valley, in the town of Calistoga.

As we approached the resort, simply to have a look for future reference, we were told by the exceedingly polite valet that the resort was only open to guests.

Then, with a large smile on his face, he asked, "Would you like an ice-cold bottle of water for the rest of your journey?"

Are you getting this?

We were lookee-loos driving an average-enough rental car.

He could have easily dismissed us as riffraff and sent us packing.

But he didn't.

Since that day, my wife has remembered that eight-ounce act of kindness.

This past week it resulted in over $5,000 in revenue for the resort, as we had a fine time celebrating our wedding anniversary at Calistoga Ranch.

Reminders for us all: never judge a book by its lookee-loo cover—and the simplest acts can pay the largest dividends.

———

**"Don't prejudge the advisor
or their practice."**
—The Millionaire Wholesaler

Your Best Client Is Their Best Prospect

I'm Rob, and I'm a recovering United Airlines Million Miler.

What have they done to wrong me?

Nothing.

It's what another has done to court and impress me.

This week, I had the great fortune of traveling to conduct a three-hour workshop at an elite meeting of eighty of the best wholesalers of a tier-one distributor.

I booked Delta as they had the best connections along with adult-size aircraft—I avoid regional jets at all costs.

Thirty minutes before takeoff, the gate agent apologetically told the packed gate area that there was a mechanical issue and departure time was pushed out forty-five minutes.

As I knew my connecting time in the megalopolis that is Atlanta was forty-one minutes, this proved problematic.

With time to kill, I tweeted my dissatisfaction.

Minutes later, @DeltaAssist tweeted back asking if they could help.

Meanwhile, I dialed the Delta Service Recovery Center eight-hundred number provided to all, as my status on Delta, well, wasn't.

I braced for the worst.

Instead I got an agent on the first ring.

She rebooked me to the next later connecting flight.

Once airborne, I noticed that the pilot was exceeding the speed limit—thereby causing us to arrive only ten minutes late.

Using in-flight Wi-Fi, I sent @DeltaAssist a message, and they rebooked me back on the earlier flight and held the later one too.

Now I'm covered six ways from Sunday, and my blood pressure never rose a point.

Impressive, Delta.

What's your competition doing to court and impress your best clients? How are you responding?

No Means No!

Raise your hand if you have flashbacks to childhood when you hear that phrase.

Maybe that's why I am so vehemently opposed to the word.

Thursday night at Gulfstream restaurant is, as my single friend Ray would say, Cougar Night.

We go to be entertained.

Recently, as the server took our order, I asked for a substitution of a side dish that came with the entrée.

The answer was no.

Remembering my disdain for the word, I went into overcome-objection mode.

"Why?" I asked.

"Policy," I was told.

Oh boy, here we go.

The manager was called and the halfhearted, nonsensical case was explained as to why the substitution could not be made.

Remaining calm, I gave my best argument (at this point it was for the sport of it) and was still told that policy prevailed.

Vowing to never return for a meal there (cocktails only and cougar viewing go together just as well), I completed my order and ate my meal.

Later, the manager returned with a twenty-five-dollar gift card apologizing for the inconvenience.

Was I pleased?

No!

This was dumb on dumber as far I could determine.

They'd prefer to abide by unintelligible policy and then monetarily apologize than find a mutually satisfactory outcome to begin with.

Great wholesalers deftly navigate the delivery of the word "no," offer alternatives, and need not offer half-baked, illogical apologies.

How do you handle the no when negotiating with financial advisors?

Is Your Internal Pitch Perfect?

Only twenty-three pitchers have tossed perfect games in Major League Baseball history.

What about your internal wholesaler's pitch?

While attending a Schwab IMPACT conference, I met an advisor who wasn't a fan of too many wholesalers. He made his opinion known via an assortment of observations and stories.

And while he was clearly scathed by bad experiences, turns out he's an accurate observer and critic of some internal wholesalers.

In fact, he sent me an MP3 of a message that an internal left for him.

Let's just say it was...rough.

In his email, the advisor commented that it, "Reminded me of a 3:00 a.m. infomercial. I thought I was getting pitched a Ronco Rotisserie."

Ouch!

Here's an idea that I successfully used with my internals: simply use your firm's voice-mail system (or iPhone Voice

Memo) to record your pitches for products, sales ideas, etc.

Have your internal listen to these pitches and nail them— just like you present them.

Two voices—one unified message.

———

"Your internal partner is your lifeline to leveraging your time and multiplying your impact."
—*The Millionaire Wholesaler*

CEO, Oh No!

"Rob, the CEO is coming to SoCal and wants to ride with you."

Panic.

Followed by anxiety.

With a side helping of fear.

That's a proper recounting of the emotions as I remember them when the then CEO of OppenheimerFunds came to visit.

As he was a high-profile industry leader, my internal and I left no stone unturned—making sure the anchor meeting of his visit, an open invitation breakfast meeting at an LAX hotel, was promoted to death.

If you were a producer, prospect, or COI, we made sure you knew about the visit...multiple times.

The venue was selected—not too expensive mind you, as this CEO was thrifty.

The catering contract with the hotel was signed.

The marketing materials were delivered.

On the day of the event, the room was carefully set for the sixty RSVPs.

Showtime!

And a grand total of twelve advisors showed up.

Twelve!

Mortified, I spent the balance of his visit apologizing, certain my budding career was about to wilt.

"Don't get down when the numbers aren't there."
—The Millionaire Wholesaler

Who Is Hubert Raudaschl?

Forgive me, but I forgot that sailing is an Olympic sport.

And, given the fact that the Opening Ceremonies are on Friday, a little Olympic trivia that you can spin into a sales idea would be in order.

You see, Austria's Hubert Raudaschl is the holder of the Olympic record for most appearances in the games.

In fact, over the years from 1964 to 1996, he appeared in nine Olympic Games.

That's what you call consistency.

Just like Hubert, great wholesalers make a name for themselves through consistency.

If there's crack in the advisor's door, the great wholesaler has a foot in it.

If the door is wide open, they capitalize on it.

If the door is closed, they keep knocking.

Consistency and wholesalers.

Goes together like United States Olympians and gold-medal performances.

———

"If you take care of the details, the numbers will take care of themselves over time."
—*The Millionaire Wholesaler*

Let the Haters Hate

Marketing your wholesaling practice is tricky.

And the more you market, the more you'll have folks who don't get your style, message, or method.

Marketing through email is trickier.

And every once in a while, I get flamed by a hater who finds the content of my Sunday Night emails irrelevant, offensive, or poorly timed, or they're just plain ticked off at the world.

Thankfully (and I am thankful), 99 percent of the feedback I get from readers about the weekly emails is incredibly positive.

But this I know—and I know it even more now after listening to a recent interview with advisors about what they want from wholesalers:

Advisors prefer email as their primary form of communication with wholesalers.

But, as the advisors on the call mentioned, they want that digital content to be relevant.

And personalized.

And insightful.

And not filled with canned garbage like too many emails in our in-boxes are filled with.

So let the haters hate.

You keep thoughtfully and creatively marketing to grow your practice.

Legends and Four-Legged Friends

Next time I'm in Chattanooga, Tennessee, I need to pay closer attention.

It seems that a legend lives there.

Luther Masingill is a DJ in town, and he's been on the air at the same radio station for seventy-two years.

A world record.

But that's not the only thing that makes him legendary.

It's the fact that for all of those years, he's been announcing lost-and-found pets on the radio.

He's reunited literally thousands of distraught owners with their four-legged best friends.

And in doing so he's built a reputation and following that no other radio personality in the state can claim.

What about your wholesaling practice?

Your reputation?

How will you be remembered?

———

"Find something that separates you from everybody else."
—*The Millionaire Wholesaler*

The One Question Ticking Off Advisors

What does that advisor think about the job you do?

Recently a survey went out to financial advisors.

It was written by us.

It was distributed by *Financial Planning* magazine.

The results were both voluminous and telling. And I'm giving you a preview of one of the most frequently commented upon issues that advisors have with us.

This one request that wholesalers make is inflaming the advisor community:

"Tell me about your business," says the wholesaler.

And the advisors in the survey say:

"Don't ask, 'Tell me about your business.' Know your niche and get to the point quickly."

—Or—

"I hate the 'Tell me about your business' question. As with most financial advisors, I'm busy, and that question requires too much time."

There are lots more—but suffice to say that we need to do more homework before the meeting and be better informed about the advisor's practice before our cheeks hit their guest chair.

———

"It's all about the client; it's never about me."
—The Millionaire Wholesaler

The Powder-Blue Wall Phone

How can you tell the real age of a house you want to buy?

Not the year it was built, because it might have been improved, but the real age.

In the case of the house that The Mrs. and I have made an offer on, there is one telling giveaway.

While the real estate agent is doing her best to sell the idea that it needs "a coat of paint and new carpet," we noticed something else.

It was indicative of the fact that the house had not been updated in any way, shape, fashion, or form in a long time—if ever.

While looking at the kitchen, once we got past the dated appliances, we noticed that there was a powder-blue telephone mounted on the wall.

Not only that, it was a powder-blue wall phone with a rotary dial!

Hello, 1972.

The house is a lot like wholesalers who fall into a state of disrepair, neglect their practice, and/or fail to upgrade to the latest technology.

How about you?

Any signs of powder-blue rotary wall phones in your practice?

Not Cut Out for Wholesaling

Bad hires.

I've made them, plenty of times.

There was the wholesaler who looked the part in the interview, was dressed to impress, and seemed knowledgeable.

When I went to ride along in the region with him, he arrived with a canvas L.L.Bean bike messenger-type briefcase slung over his shoulder.

That first morning of our time together, we hailed a cab in New York City; I slid in first, and he and his bag followed—spilling coffee from his premeeting Starbucks all over my suit.

His brief tenure went downhill from there.

Then there was the wholesaler whom I hired to work in a multistate region, who I knew was green and trainable.

The problem was he was so afraid of flying that he needed his meds to survive the flight.

I had visions of him nodding off in the advisor's waiting area, drooling on the couch pillows.

He resigned after ninety days.

And to this day my former employees give me a hard time about the divisional sales manager I hired who turned out to be so bad that he was hired and fired in less than ninety days.

Every time a seemingly good hire went bad, I was reminded of the symphony of extraordinary characteristics that truly great wholesalers possess.

The Wholesaling Marathon

Valuable lessons.

We've all learned them.

Back at the beginning of my wholesaling career, there was a manager (Anne) who asked if I could do a meeting on a Friday.

My (dumbest possible) answer was, "Fridays are my office days. I don't do appointments."

As I was new on her wholesaling scene, Anne decided to call my boss and vent her displeasure with my answer.

Thankfully, rather than ripping me a new one, my boss explained that Anne had a history of volatility.

And then she said something that resonated loudly.

"Build the best relationship with Anne that you can...and, the fact is, you will outlast her in this business."

Whoa!

Sound advice.

Sure enough, less than a year later, Anne was gone—and did not resurface in my wholesaling world.

She was built to run a one-hundred-meter race.

I was learning to run the marathon called wholesaling.

How's your race being run?

———

"Don't let rejection impact you."
—*The Millionaire Wholesaler*

A Moment of Wholesaling Zen

"Sometimes the first duty of intelligent men is the restatement of the obvious."—George Orwell

Have you ever had a wholesaling epiphany?

You know, one where you smack yourself upside your own head and think, "Geez, that was obvious."

One of many that I recall was speaking with an advisor with my big ass paper calendar (remember those?) opened, ready to schedule our next meeting, client event, or social outing.

I always felt compelled to explain why a date in my calendar worked or didn't.

Or, if it was an advisor that I was not really looking forward to scheduling an event with, I'd feel a pang of guilt—as if they could see that Tuesday the eighth was wide open—when I said no to the date.

And then one day the obvious hit me.

"Hey, dummy," I said to myself, "they can't actually see your calendar."

Seriously people, this moment of Zen changed my wholesaling world.

It made it OK to schedule the right people, in the right order and at the right time, in a way that suited my calendar.

Now you may be a whole lot smarter than me when it comes to obvious stuff, but I know that wholesalers always need great time management and organization tips.

———

"Be extremely organized and focused when you are working."
—*The Millionaire Wholesaler*

It Worked So Well I Stopped Doing It

It's true—I have Shiny Object Syndrome (SOS).

The three most pronounced symptoms of SOS are:

1. Easily distracted by new ideas/concepts/strategies.

2. Tempted by the latest trend/guru/technique.

3. A tendency to leave behind tried-and-true methods that worked well and were successful for the business, in favor of the latest and greatest.

And, as a recovering sufferer of SOS, I need to make sure that there is balance between the adoption of new and the adherence to that which is tried and true.

This reminder of SOS comes to mind because over the last few weeks I have had coaching client discussions that go like this:

Me: Does the idea we discussed resonate with you?

Client: It does—in fact, it's a lot like something I used to do.

Me: It worked so well that you stopped.

Client: Exactly.

Do you suffer from SOS in your wholesaling practice?

His Secret to Success

Comedy is a slippery slope.

Especially flight attendant comedy.

And if you have flown Southwest before you know that there's always the flight attendant that makes a valiant, albeit half-baked, attempt at humor.

Frequently it's just not that funny, you know?

This flight was different.

This flight had Chris.

Chris was on top of his game in a big way.

Every single passenger was greeted at the door.

He helped folks find space for their luggage.

He was exceedingly polite.

And he was damn funny.

At each opportunity that he had to speak to the passengers, he was in entertainment mode.

He even had a song that he sang (yes, sang) as we taxied to the gate upon arrival.

After which most of the plane applauded.

He was so good at what he did that two passengers commented that, "It's the only flight we've ever been on that we didn't want to end!"

When asked why he was so enthusiastic he said, "My secret to success is that I love my job, and I love people—that makes it easy."

Memorable indeed.

Fifteen Wholesaler Sales Rules

These fifteen Wholesaler Sales Rules were written ten-plus years ago for a new sales team I was starting.

They're every bit as relevant today as the day I wrote them:

1. Don't just be on time, be early.

2. Trite but true: underpromise and overdeliver...every time.

3. If they ask for one of something, send them two.

4. If they want it in two days, send it in one.

5. No sale will ever compromise your integrity.

6. No salesperson needs to work with abusive (verbal or otherwise) clients. Fire them.

7. Remove "no," "can't," "won't," etc. from your vocabulary.

8. Be the best-dressed/most immaculately groomed person at every client meeting. They will notice.

9. Be a student of the market/business. If you don't subscribe to and read *The Wall Street Journal*, *Forbes*,

Fortune, Money, Smart Money, Kiplinger's, the *New York Times*, not to mention a host of blogs, start today.

10. Always look for the lighter/brighter side. If you're not having fun and laughing along the way, we need to talk.

11. Have you hugged your internal sales partner/admin today, telephonically speaking of course?

12. Expand your vocabulary and the clarity of your voice. I may not be the smartest guy around, but I might sound like it!

13. Simple math: Salesperson Listen to Talk Ratio = 2:1.

14. Creativity sells. Feeling brain dead? Let's brainstorm.

15. Be the best-prepared salesperson in your territory. If you're winging it you better be really good...or lucky.

Be a Wholesaling Hero

One hundred years' worth of amazing lessons.

That's what it feels like after only five years in Entrepreneurial America.

And the relatable message to your wholesaling practice is this:

If you want to build someone's loyalty quickly and impressively, come to their rescue.

Be a hero when a hero is in need.

The quick story:

Twenty-three days before we are set to go to press for the Fall 2012 issue of I Carry The Bag magazine, we terminated our relationship with our graphic designer.

In a mad scramble to find a suitable replacement, we reached out to four designers.

Designer #1—no email reply after three days.

Designer #2—no email reply after two days.

Designer #3—Prompt reply but wanted to upsell us for more services.

Designer #4—Returned our outreach in under four hours, scheduled a phone call to better understand our predicament/requirements, and found a way to get our immediate need handled (at an acceptable price point) before worrying about the next phase of the relationship.

Clearly Designer #4 gets the whole hero idea.

So the next time you get a call from an advisor in need, see if you can be her hero.

Then watch the relationship blossom.

———

"You've always got to be willing to go above and beyond to help an advisor."

—The Millionaire Wholesaler

A Very Good Question

"What one quality is universal among the most successful wholesalers whom you coach?"

That question was asked of me at the end of a fantastic wholesaler session in Charleston, South Carolina, this week.

It was asked by the divisional manager on behalf of the attendees in the room.

As I stood at the front of the room, I thought for only a moment and then offered the thoughts I briefly recap here.

The most successful wholesalers I coach are:

Curious: the best clients always want to know more—and are always questioning best practices.

Discontented: in this case meaning they are not complacent—they are always sharpening the saw.

Doers: they act. They don't say that they will act and don't...they commit to a task or a challenge, and they act.

How curious are you?

Are you developing "complacency creep"?

Do you do or simply say you'll do?

———

"We cannot confuse busy work with productive activity."

—The Millionaire Wholesaler

So Not a Lady's Man

Personal question:

How did you fare with the opposite sex during your high-school years?

I was a train wreck.

You know that whole notion of playing it cool and taking your time while courting?

I was clueless.

My heart was on my sleeve, and I simply tried too hard.

And apparently some wholesalers today are doing the same thing.

On a recent Wholesaler Masterminds Group Coaching call, one of the participants, a long-tenured and most successful wholesaler offered, "My advisors have commented recently that newer wholesalers in the region are simply trying too hard—they expect to be best friends with advisors almost immediately."

"Wholesalers need to relax and let the 'game' come to them," he said.

Makes perfect sense when you consider it in the context of all of our relationships that matter.

They don't happen overnight.

They happen over time.

———

"Have a great work ethic, be trustworthy and be confident in yourself."
—*The Millionaire Wholesaler*

The Frankenstorm of Wholesaler Data

Circa 1992 a FedEx package arrived on my doorstep every Friday.

It came from my firm's home office and had all the latest info on our products, manager updates, rep lists, etc.—all in printed word.

It took about two hours to wade through it.

And that was the extent of the data flow from the home office.

Today's wholesaler is drowned with data, which if printed would wrap around the earth multiple times.

So how do you keep up with it all?

One idea: change your perspective on how you view the data.

Is it *all* designed to be consumed within days of receipt?

Or is it like the Internet?

Rather than trying to read all the data the Internet provides (an impossible task), you consume the data that the Internet has to offer when you need to access the bytes of info that help you succeed at the task you are undertaking.

Today's wholesaler is getting soaked in a downpour of data.

Perhaps a different approach to how it's all consumed will make it a bit less scary.

———

"Get better organized with new technology."
—The Millionaire Wholesaler

One-Hit Wonders

As I built my book of sellers for OppenheimerFunds, I was tenacious and persistent.

The more a prospect offered resistance, the harder I sold.

Dan was a broker I called on frequently.

He was a massive producer and wrote almost none of my product.

For years, I diligently called on Dan each time I came through his city.

Each time Dan promised to review the material, present a product, and order a hypo—something, anything.

The "competitive me" knew I had to slay this dragon.

Dan was going to be a top producer.

Or not.

After three years of beating my head against the wall (hey, I'm a little slow), I finally cut bait and took Dan out of the rotation—he was wasting my time.

I had allowed the chase of the big producer to cloud my judgment.

Looking back, I know that I let this pattern repeat itself too.

And that's the deceptive sales trap.

Try this as you plan for the year ahead: go through your list of prospects and one-hit wonders and figure out how many you have presented to, followed up with, and heard false promises from.

Then, make a hard and important decision to just stop.

The competitive you will get over the letdown.

Your next top producers are just ahead.

And now you'll have more time to devote to them because you're not wasting time.

———

"Don't try to fit a square peg in a round hole. You can't work with every advisor successfully."
—*The Millionaire Wholesaler*

Hold Me Closer, Tony Danza

Ever see a service or product and think, "Why didn't I think of that?"

One example of this is the original Smiley Face.

For more than forty years, we have all heard the lament from family and friends that this should have been "their" idea.

Another example for folks like me who always screw up song lyrics is the official misheard lyrics book *Hold Me Closer, Tony Danza.*

Then there's the same book we've run across in almost every Napa winery titled *Wine Dogs.*

Seems that a guy came through the Valley and started taking pictures of every dog at every vineyard he could find.

The dog owners were only too delighted to have their dog featured in the book, and the book is now for sale in every single one of those wineries.

Brilliant.

As you think ahead to your business plan, make sure you leave room for innovation.

How will you create a process, perspective, or pitch that has other wholesalers wondering, "Why didn't I think of that?"

———

"You need to constantly reinvent yourself."

—The Millionaire Wholesaler

Don't Burn Your Bird

At the ripe old age of twenty-two, I found myself working as a headhunter.

My job was to place financial services professionals in banking.

And thirty years ago, not dissimilar from today, banking was a conservative sector in which to work.

But I was too young to know that.

So in the week that proceeded Thanksgiving of that year, I called all my HR contacts with only one purpose.

I gave them the phone number for the Butterball Turkey Talk-Line.

Because, I offered, "I don't want you to burn your bird."

The reaction of the HR reps was one of pleasant surprise.

They appreciated the humor and found it refreshing that someone was taking a novel approach.

Ah, youth.

I was young enough to not know "the rules."

Turns out it was a most memorable thing to do and great for future business.

How are you developing your MQ—Memorability Quotient®?

Hire with Reservations

I sat at my dining room table overcome with anxiety.

The thing that stood between me and my first wholesaling gig was the personality assessment.

Damn! I hated these things.

Years before, I had been denied a position as a wirehouse advisor trainee strictly because of an assessment.

And the assessment in front of me was particularly insidious, as it asked the usual psychoanalytical questions you'd expect and also tested my general intellect.

Fortunately this was an "open-book" assessment, and I got to take my time, use various lifelines, and double-check my answers.

By the time I got to the last question, I felt confident that I would not have another position slip away based on some evil algorithm.

Yes, I did get the gig.

Yes, I found great success.

And yes, years later I learned that the assessment returned a recommendation to the hiring manager.

For me it read "Hire with reservations."

Hire with reservations?

Evil assessments.

Always Pack Your Rubbers

Born in New York.

But raised in Miami.

With thirty-five years in SoCal.

Let's just say that I'm not a huge fan of the elements.

Or, said another way, I'm a weather wimp.

So it stands to reason that on a visit to ride along with my Upstate New York wholesaler, in winter, I packed my rubbers.

Oh, you may call them "overshoes," but I just wanted to keep my $300 Ferragamos dry and free of road salt.

What a mistake.

I would have been better off wearing full-fledged snow boots with my suit—because I took a serious dose of pain from my wholesaler.

It was a not-so-subtle combination of East Coast, in your face, fashion harassment and thinly veiled sarcasm.

In fact, I take crap from him to this day—some ten years later.

Management—a humbling experience.

———

"You have to be prepared to be a good wholesaler."

—The Millionaire Wholesaler

No More Lumps of Coal

I'm not a hillbilly.

Yet my first holiday working as a wholesaler for a New York firm was an eye opener.

Maybe it was the lavish party at the Vista Hotel at the World Trade Center.

Or the general spirit of the holidays that pervades Manhattan.

But I'm thinking it was the newfound phenomenon called the Holiday Bonus Check.

"What did your last firm offer for a holiday bonus," asked my new boss.

"A supermarket gift certificate for a turkey," I replied.

And she laughed.

And laughed.

And she's laughing as she reads this today.

When the check came, I knew I had made the right career decision.

A decision that has been fiscally validated in every year since that first bonus.

We have much to be grateful for in our business.

I hope your year in review supports that thought.

———

"Live well below your means, don't mistake rising sales with sales genius; and save for a rainy day."
—*The Millionaire Wholesaler*

Lucky to Be Alive

Yes, lucky.

That's how I felt after a visit to ride with a wholesaler in New York.

As we screamed up the Bronx River Parkway in route to the next meeting, he had a huge Automobile Club map opened across the entire dashboard and me.

Did I mention that the car was moving?

Did I mention that we were going at least 130 miles per hour—or so it seemed?

Apparently he had not dialed in the exact location of the next meeting before we got in the car.

And, as he drove with his knee while looking at the map, he had obviously forgotten the drivers' ed mantra.

Ten and two.

It's also a great metaphor for the year ahead: steer your upcoming Career Year not with your knee but with your wholesaling hands placed firmly on your practice, at ten and two.

But I'm Older than Most Rare Scotch

As a flyer with access to airline clubs (read: free cocktails), I spent part of a recent delay at the bar.

And I witnessed a range in human behavior that began with the bartenders being required to ask for ID from everyone—regardless of the patron's apparent age.

The Indignant: Those angered and annoyed by what they perceived as unfair treatment.

They emitted the "How could you possibly be asking me for an ID—don't you know who I am?" vibe.

The Resigned: Those who simply accepted the request.

Their attitude was, "Hey, if that's what standing between me and my Cabernet, no problem."

The Elated: Those (like me) who were more than glad to prove they were over twenty-one, though it's painfully, absurdly obvious.

They simply produced their driver's license or passport, smiled, and said, "Thanks! You've made my day."

As I watched the thirsty masses and their reactions, I was reminded that we all have a choice about the attitude that we display.

———

"Be an optimist."
—The Millionaire Wholesaler

That Sucking Sound You Hear

Sometimes remarks stay with me like the indelible tomato sauce stain from the last Italian meal I ate.

And so it is that a comment made by a wirehouse COI during an interview for *I Carry The Bag*, had rattled around my head for months.

He said, "I consider time spent with wholesalers a time debit."

Really?

His experience is such that when a wholesaler approaches his office, the sucking sound he hears is that of time that he will never get back?

Truly sad.

Make it your mission to bring ideas, concepts, questions, insights, observations, and assistance that will allow you to win over even the most cynical COI.

And be sure to demonstrate your PVP—Peerless Value Proposition®.

Because you should never be viewed as a time debit.

Ever.

———

**"You have got to be able to
bring something other than product to
the table."**
—*The Millionaire Wholesaler*

Simply Walking His Lama

Oh, the things we see while on the road.

Be it the road that takes you to the next borough.

Or the road that leads to the furthest, most distant state you cover.

The first time I saw the snowcapped mountains surrounding Seattle in winter, or the flat out gorgeous beauty of Kalispell, Montana, I knew this was one terrific perk of the job.

But not all sights are as easily explained.

Like the time I was speaking to DeeAnne.

Who was out wholesaling in Los Angeles's San Fernando Valley when I called.

And, while speaking to me, she described watching a man taking his pet lama for a walk down the street.

Of course, that show ended when the man and the lama turned into a storefront.

A storefront for a tattoo and piercing parlor.

You can't make this stuff up.

Who Killed Mo?

Best January ever!

Those were the words that a private-coaching client spoke this past week.

And, as is the case with my terrific clients, he wanted to discuss how not to lose the significant momentum he had built up.

So what kills momentum, you ask?

Lots of things actually—but here are a few that should be high on your watch list:

Complacency creep—it's way too easy to let success breed the insidious behavior that accompanies complacency.

Never get too fat nor too happy with your success.

Process interruptions—beware the "it worked so well that I stopped" phenomenon.

Your email campaigns, follow-up process, and thank-you cards (to name a few) helped get you to here.

Don't stop now.

Ego overload—we are only as good as our last meeting, our last seminar, or our last month's production.

"Where ego, I go too" can empower us—and also bite us in the butt.

Stay humble and thankful.

You got Mo?

Don't kill it.

———

"Check your ego at the door."
—The Millionaire Wholesaler

Just One Great Idea

You are not like everyone else.

What appeals to me may repulse you.

Then why do we lump all advisors into the same marketing pile?

As I interviewed a recent guest expert on the *Wholesaler Masterminds Radio* podcast, he spoke about the importance of customization.

And how repeatedly doing things the same way and expecting a different outcome defines insanity—to paraphrase Albert Einstein.

So why do we send the same trinket to all producers?

Or the same PDF about the same product?

Try this:

1. Divide your Top 100 advisors into categories based on their general interests—golf nuts, foodies, etc.

2. Create a tag in your CRM for each advisor based on their interest category.

3. The next time you see a post, article, or gift idea, sort your Top 100 by the interest tag that you created and personalize a quick message that accompanies what you're sending.

It's a fantastic way to cut through the wholesaling Sea of Sameness.

And a surefire way to increase your MQ—Memorability Quotient®.

———

"Do things other wholesalers won't do."

—The Millionaire Wholesaler

Thank God for Mistakes

As mentioned here previously, The Mrs. and I are preparing for a move.

And that means combing through and cleaning the closet in my office.

Scary thought.

Since that is where the mistakes are buried.

Like the five hundred one-sheets I long ago had printed for my new business.

Since it's a digital world, I've used perhaps thirty of the printed versions.

Or the audio demo CDs I had prepared for prospecting at a conference.

Bad idea.

So I say TGFM: Thank God for Mistakes.

Because every mistake I uncovered reminded me of the lesson I learned.

And today's great wholesalers learn from their mistakes.

"The successful man will profit from his mistakes and try again in a different way." —Dale Carnegie

How many mistakes are lurking in your office?

What have you learned from them?

Overpaid Wholesalers

Journalists can be really irritating.

The Mrs. recently asked if I saw the article about the "10 Most Overpaid Jobs" in America.

As I smoothed down my neck hairs from standing straight on end, I opened the link she forwarded.

In true uninformed journalistic prose, I read:

Wholesaler, financial services ($109,000). Is one insurance policy or mutual fund really that much better than another? The sales pros who pitch financial products to businesses (which might offer them to their own employees or customers, in turn) strive to make their offerings seem best, but skepticism is an occupational hazard in this job.

It seems that @rickjnewman of *U.S. News & World Report* has thrown facts to the wind considering two of his other ten jobs on the list are investment consultant and portfolio analyst.

The big takeaway—aside from the ignorance of the journalist?

If you are wholesaling for $109,000 a year, you need to start a job search—today.

Ship to Nowhere

The advisor day cruise to Ensenada that I helped sponsor was pure high-sea torture.

I vowed never to set foot aboard a ship again.

Recently I violated that vow by touring the Queen Mary.

This floating museum honors one of the great passenger ships that ever sailed by preserving the stories and the technology of the past.

Among the relics on display was a large cord board that served as the main telephone switchboard of the ship.

Operators sat at the board and assisted parties that wished to speak with each other by patching one phone line's cord into another—physically connecting the conversation.

An elegant communication technology in a much simpler era.

Today, with the nonstop connectivity of smartphones, we risk getting lulled into thinking that text can replace conversations.

And in doing so a nuance is lost.

And so might the real meaning of your intended message.

Wholesaling is a craft that requires keen communication skills.

To rely too heavily on the typewritten word may inadvertently send your practice on a misdirected journey.

———

"The modes and methods of communication have to be different for every individual."
—*The Millionaire Wholesaler*

The One with the Knicks' Cheerleaders

VIP tickets to the Knicks.

Dinner before in the Madison Square Garden Club.

Meet and greet with Willis Reed.

Photo op with Knicks' cheerleaders.

T-shirts for all.

Sweatshirts for all.

Can I recall what firms' advisors were there?

No.

Am I certain that the event was worth the exorbitant price of admission?

Heck no.

Do I still have the picture taken with the cheerleaders?

Well, yes.

Sometimes we spend wads of money to impress our advisors and create MQ—Memorability Quotient®—moments.

Often the memorable moments are created by far more simple things.

How do you take the day-to-day events of wholesaling and make them most memorable?

———

"It's not how great your product is—it's how focused you are."

—*The Millionaire Wholesaler*

Are You the Real Thing?

Quiz time.

Q: What's the most recognized word in the world?

A: OK.

Q: What's the second-most recognized?

A: Coca-Cola

Amazing, right?

The Coke brand is so ubiquitous that you can go to almost any corner of the earth, say the magic word, and be clearly understood.

Q: What soda brand was founded before Coke and led in market share before the Great Depression?

A: Moxie

The problem was Moxie lost their market-leading position during the Great Depression because they pulled back on their advertising.

What's the lesson for us?

You can never take your foot off of the territory marketing accelerator.

The moment you do, your competitor may well become the real thing.

———

"Never stop working—stay active and see the right number of people."
—The Millionaire Wholesaler

Of Wholesalers and U-Hauls

Five hundred fifty-two miles.

That was the total distance driven last weekend in the move to Northern California.

But unlike an ordinary drive at seventy-plus miles per hour, this drive was with a U-Haul trailer in tow.

Which meant traveling decidedly slower.

In the slow lane.

A place where my lead foot and I are not used to being.

Aside from the humbling experience of having every other car on the road scream past at Indy raceway speeds, here's my biggest discovery about slow-lane driving.

The slow lane is where the road is the roughest and majority of the potholes are.

And as my U-Haul and I bounced along the rutted road, I couldn't help but think about the wholesaler who is stuck in the slow lane.

Unwilling or unable to speed up their practice because of the stuff they're hauling around.

Perhaps content with the competition screaming past them.

Once the trip was complete and the U-Haul was unhitched, I got back to the more comfortable lane that great wholesalers enjoy.

Leading from in front—in the fast lane.

I Didn't Know What I Didn't Know

"I work with wholesalers all the time, so I know what the job entails," said the misguided job applicant.

And that's the thing—folks on the outside assume they know what this job is all about.

I know I thought I knew.

But boy, did I have it wrong.

And so do the unknowing observers of the craft.

There are not many careers that call for you to be proficient at all of the following—often all in the same appointment:

Ambassador
Coach
Confidant
Teacher
Motivator
Negotiator
Jester
Analyst
Mentor
Futurist
Entertainer
_____ (fill in yours here)

But in order for you to have your Career Year, it's inevitable that one of more of these skills needs refining.

What will you commit to improving upon this week?

Just Give It to Me Straight

Ah, rental living!

It's been almost twenty-five years since I was at the mercy of a landlord.

And for the next ninety days, I am once again.

Prior to my arrival, the landlord says, "We are building a new fence for the property—should be done in a week; is that OK?"

[Raise your hand if you share my skepticism.]

Me: "Sure, as long as it's not going to take longer."

Day of arrival at rental, this exchange with contractor:

Me: "How long before you are done?"

Contractor: "We should be done by the end of the week."

[Do you see the pattern developing here?]

Me: "Great, as long as it doesn't take longer."

Now in week three, the sound of generators and nail guns has replaced the chirping of birds.

And it reminds me how important transparency is for great wholesalers.

Tell advisors the unvarnished truth—about performance, service issues, missed deadlines, etc. and you'll strengthen the bond.

BS your way through, out of fear or neglect, and you'll trash your relationships.

———

"Tragic wholesaler mistake: not being about full disclosure."
—*The Millionaire Wholesaler*

Own It Like Nancy

Twenty-six miles north lies the town of Middletown—in the middle of nowhere.

Screaming past on Highway 29, we noticed ten to twelve cars pulled off to the side of the road near a sign that read, "Yard Sale."

The Mrs. and I couldn't resist the gravitational pull of a country road lined with other people's treasures.

At the back of the property, there was a nondescript shed filled with bad art work hanging on the walls.

In through a side door appeared a woman in a straw cowboy hat and apron and with a big smile.

From behind the table at the back of the shed, she exclaimed to all three visitors, "Welcome. I'm Nancy, and I'm the curator of the art you see here."

Curator?

People, this was not The Met or MOMA.

Yet Curator Nancy proudly described all the goodness that her small assortment of art had to offer.

Nancy owned her pitch.

And her pitch was rock solid.

Wholesalers who convey the same self-assuredness in their presentations always crush it.

———

"Have a great work ethic, be trustworthy and be confident in yourself."
—*The Millionaire Wholesaler*

The Habitual Wholesaler

Leave the house.

Arrive at new office.

Turn on computer.

Walk ½ block to coffee shop.

Buy large coffee.

Walk back to office.

This is the new habit that I have formed in only the last thirty days here in a brand new environment.

Habits are formed through a process called "context-dependent repetition."

In this case the context (arriving at work) is linking to the response that becomes the habit (walking to the coffee shop).

And the experts often say it only takes twenty-one days to form any habit.

So in the next twenty-one days, you can decide to form a new habit that will catapult your practice in the second half of this Career Year.

Or you can choose to do the same things over and over and wonder why the results have not changed.

"Insanity: doing the same thing over and over again and expecting different results." —*Albert Einstein*

In Search of Cockeyed Millstones

It's easy for us to be misunderstood.

Or to misunderstand.

For example, somewhere in history the term "cockeyed" got defined as foolish, askew, or intoxicated.

Yet if you were a miller, instead of a wholesaler, and made your living grinding other people's corn and wheat, you'd know what "cockeyed" really meant.

The perfect balance of the gristmill's upper stone (sitting on a pin called a cock) resting only sheets of paper distance atop the lower stone perfectly positioned in a divot called the eye.

Hence, to the miller, to be cockeyed is to make certain your stones don't wobble (which just sounds painful)—as wobbly stones will spark and blow up your mill.

Are your messages to advisors being misunderstood?

Are you listening and clarifying in your advisor meetings in a way that avoids misunderstanding?

It would be a shame if your business blew up due to wobbly stones.

Better to be cockeyed, right?

———

**"Listening is such a huge part of
what we do."**
—*The Millionaire Wholesaler*

Shantytown Cabernet, Anyone?

I love wine.

I buy too much to keep at home.

In my old neighborhood, I rented a storage locker that kept the precious contents at just the right temperature and humidity.

And it was in a facility that resembled a shantytown.

It was a collection of odd-sized, barely standing, and questionably secure plywood units.

Naturally, after moving, I needed a home for the liquid gold.

The new facility looked as if it had been built only yesterday—sterile enough to perform a minor surgery in.

Security was so tight that I had to pick a gate password that I have since forgotten.

It also came equipped with concierges who helped you move your cases in and out of your locker.

Seriously?

Concierges?

This new facility did the same exact thing as the old one—it kept the contents safe and sound.

But it offered a whole different experience that blew my mind.

What about your region?

You have the same product (more or less) as the next wholesaler.

How can you make the experience more memorable?

Life in Mayberry

Small-town life is sure different than New York, Miami, or Los Angeles.

And lest you think that I now resort to benign statements of the obvious, let me explain.

This week we went to the local movie theater.

It has but one screen and 155 seats and has three shows per day.

It's also a social center of the community.

While at the Cinevision MegaPlex Ultra 36, located at the local big-city mall, folks talk in hushed tones while waiting for the movie to start; here in Mayberry it's social hour.

Members of the community catching up on the latest how-do-you-dos before the start of the show.

It got me thinking about communities.

What thread of commonality can you string through a group that allows you to build upon it with ideas and information that let you to serve the community in a valuable way?

Advisors who are former college athletes—because you were too.

Advisors who all have CFAs—because you do too.

Advisors who all love to fish—because it's your passion too.

What community can you build with your advisors?

Some Things Aren't Negotiable

It was bound to happen.

On the highway between here and there is a bunch of road construction.

And last weekend a rogue rock attacked my windshield.

In search of repair, to stop the spread of the spidery blemish, I called a local service.

A new business that started just this year.

Their outgoing voice-mail message was simply the Verizon computerized automaton most of us know.

When we spoke, I asked the owner why he chose this generic message versus the name of his business, his own voice, or anything that would be better than what he had.

His answer took me aback.

"I'm not very computer literate and couldn't figure out how to change it," he said.

To be in business, some things are simply table stakes.

Knowing how to navigate technology in 2013 is not negotiable.

And in this business's case, it will likely cause their demise by 2014.

What about your practice?

Do you merely tolerate technology or leverage it to its fullest?

———

"Embrace technology."
—*The Millionaire Wholesaler*

Food for Thought

Great restaurants abound.

Some have menus as long as your firm's latest white paper.

As I read page upon page of epicurean possibilities, my mind simply ceases to function.

My ability to decide comes to a screeching halt.

The same is true for a wholesaler's product pitch.

Some wholesalers insist on flooding the advisor with the entire contents of their bag—pitching virtually everything.

And doing so compels the advisor to sell nothing.

The great wholesaler understands the paradox of all that choice and opts to keep the twenty- to forty-five-minute discussion concise and laser focused.

How tasty is your pitch?

————

"I always try to put myself on the other side of the desk, and think, 'what can I say to this person?'"
—*The Millionaire Wholesaler*

The Real Decision Maker?

"We need to install a _____; where do you want it placed?" said the general contractor.

"Wrong department," I said.

If you ask me where it should be hung, what color it should be, what direction it should slide, and so forth, I'll offer you my mantra for the last six months of home renovation:

"Wrong department—not my decision."

My job is to be the enforcer and write checks.

All other decisions are left in far more capable hands—The Mrs.

Are you sure the prospects you are speaking to actually make their own product decisions?

Or are they influenced by the home office, local management, senior advisor, or other entity that will have your pitch fall on deaf ears?

Finding the real decision maker in my house is easy.

Just locate the beautiful five-foot-three blond woman.

Who's the real decision maker in your prospect's practice?

———

"See the right people—and see them often enough."

—*The Millionaire Wholesaler*

Half a Wholesaler

Typical male.

Very few needs.

Give me a comfortable couch.

A big-screen TV.

And superfast Wi-Fi.

So when I learned that Armando was wiring the new home with Cat 5, Cat 6, and HDMI, I was pumped—never mind the fact that I have no idea what these are!

This week was the installation of the whole system, and I'm delighted...with half the outcome.

The problem was Armando was half a professional.

While his technical skills were excellent and he had great attention to detail, his organizational skills sucked.

As the owner of his business, he spent half of his day answering phone calls and responding to emails while on my job, resulting in the job taking twice as long.

His ability to communicate his ideas and solutions was poor—he simply didn't command his messaging.

What about your practice?

Where do you need to improve?

Are you only half the wholesaler you should be?

———

"Get an organizational method that works for you that will continue to keep your schedule full."
—The Millionaire Wholesaler

Truth or Consequences

The truth, the whole truth, and nothing but the truth.

Isn't that what we all expect?

We have a reader of the Sunday Night Email who calls offenders in our business "half-salers"—wholesalers who only speak half the truth.

Why is it that all too often we get less than all of the truth?

Is it because the offender doesn't have the bravery to speak the whole truth?

Example: General Contractor says: "I'll be out on Thursday."

That was part of the truth.

The whole truth was that he left on Thursday, wasn't due back until the following Tuesday, and was unreachable because he was in Cabo San Lucas!

Did I mention that his tequila-fest coincided with the final two days of a seven-month project?

"Three things cannot be long hidden: the sun, the moon, and the truth." —Buddha

Half-salers, beware.

———

"Being brutally honest; I think you gain so much traction rather than misleading people."

—The Millionaire Wholesaler

You Take Care of the Numbers

I was a whiner.

Early on in my sales career, I frequently complained whenever business was slow.

How there wasn't the right return coming from my efforts?

One day I whined my way into my boss's office.

"It's so slow."

"Sales aren't coming."

"Maybe I'm no good at this gig," were all versions of my whine du jour.

And then he said the phrase that has stuck for the last thirty-plus years.

"You take care of the numbers, and the numbers will take care of you."

So when you are feeling a bit sales stuck, as if the efforts you extend are not resulting in the sales that you expect, just keep taking care of the numbers.

See the right advisors.

Deliver the right message.

With the right frequency.

And know that the numbers will take care of you.

Long Day's Journey

An eight-minute drive to airport.

The valet parks the car.

Blissfully short security lines.

A total of fourteen potential departure gates.

That was then.

This is now:

Eighty-four-minute drive to off-site parking.

Security lines for as far as the eye can see.

GPS required to locate the departure gate.

Yet, with similar repeatable processes in place (emphasis on repeatable), even this new journey becomes less frenetic, more predictable, and far less stressful.

Kind of like a great wholesaler's practice.

When was the last time you reflected on your repeatable processes?

Because you never know when your journey may change.

———

"Have a process for how you wholesale."
—*The Millionaire Wholesaler*

Internals, Port, and Cigars

Sixty-dollar glasses of port.

Thirty-five dollar cigars.

Fond memories of 57 E. 57th Street.

To the well-heeled wholesaler traveler, this address can only mean the Four Seasons NYC.

And to me and my internals, circa 1992–1998, it meant one of the best bonding experiences known to distribution-kind.

Our dedicated server at the Bar was Kim, and thru her good graces, we slipped past any velvet rope straight to a reserved table.

My internals then, not unlike many internals today, had not yet had the opportunity to experience this slice of the good life.

And the fact that we shared the experience had two distinct benefits:

1. As they wanted to become externals, this gave them a financial taste of what was to come.

2. There's just something about great atmosphere and rare libations, and in that day, a killer Arturo Fuente that made the bonding process effortless.

These internals went on to become some of the most successful externals in the business.

What sort of relationship are you forging with your internal wholesaler?

———

"My internal is number one."
—The Millionaire Wholesaler

Trouble at WTC

Q. What do you get when you take thirty advisors from one broker dealer and fly them all to New York City?

A. A hard lesson learned.

Why, you ask?

Well, it wasn't because of the incredible welcome event that was held 107 floors above Manhattan at Windows on the World.

Nor was it because of my performance at the event; even as a brand new wholesaler, I was an engaging host.

Apparently the problem, as my boss so clearly explained the next day, was my decision to take the whole crew out for post-event touring and cocktails.

And getting in way too late that night.

Or was it morning?

As a master of the obvious, I knew the boss was ticked off by the door that slammed upon my entry to her office.

And by that unique shade of red her face had turned.

"Experience is simply the name we give our mistakes."
—Oscar Wilde

Oh, Those Tricky Marketers!

I feel cheated.

Is it my imagination, or are things shrinking?

While much has changed here recently, the need to shower has not.

Ergo, the urgent need for soap.

A quick swing through the local Rite Aid, three bars of Coast soap in hand, and on with the rest of the day.

But wait.

While the exterior packaging looks the same, the bars themselves have a large concave chunk contoured out.

Oh, the marketers will say it offers a "better soaping experience."

Or, depending on the shrunken new product, that the smaller version is "greener," or more "portable" or "healthier."

But all I see is a smaller bar, which costs more, than the last incarnation of the brand.

In a world where we are asked to accept less for more, you have a golden opportunity to be memorable by simply adding more real value.

So what's your MQ—Memorability Quotient®?

———

"In order: sell yourself, sell the company, sell the product."
—The Millionaire Wholesaler

Wholesalers' Pain in the But

What's one of the most insidious words in our wholesaling vocabulary?

The one that is stealthily deceitful because it sounds innocent—yet hardly ever is.

Because it deflects the user's accountability, attempting to shift blame to anyone else.

Or it immediately sounds confrontational.

Or it implies that I wasn't listening to what you said.

The word, which once eradicated from use, changes the trajectory of a conversation.

A word that great wholesalers are better served without.

But.

"Yes, but..." [infers there are negative conditions].

"Good thoughts, but..." [suggests that I don't agree with any of them].

"We can have there by Wednesday, but..." [the commitment may not stick].

What's a simple replacement?

Next time, intentionally replace the word "but" with the word "and."

Try it.

The Wholesaler Who's Waiting

Some wholesalers spend their entire careers waiting.

Waiting for the better job to move to.

Waiting for the "next" career after this one.

Waiting for vacation, holiday, or a personal day to take time off.

Waiting to amass more money.

Waiting for a more solid home life.

Waiting, and assuring themselves it will come, for a time to be happier.

Waiting to get inspired, take action, create a plan, and divine the "answer."

And then they blink, and they waited too long.

So if you want to do or be, go do or be.

Just don't wait.

———

"Every year is a marathon and too many wholesalers get burned out because they don't have balance."
—*The Millionaire Wholesaler*

It's All About the Recovery

That hairline crack at the top of the newly installed custom cabinet wasn't a crack at all.

The interesting shadow cast on the wall in the setting sun was no shadow.

It was black mold.

Caused by the leak in the toilet one floor above.

The toilet that the plumber didn't install correctly.

And was issue number I've lost count that this subcontractor caused in a brand new home.

While it would seem reasonable that my blood pressure would be 240/stroke, it's not.

The reason has to do with the manner in which the general contractor has handled the issues.

The leak was discovered at 5:20 p.m.

By 5:40 p.m. his guys were at my door to diagnose and formulate a game plan for repair.

Screw-ups, both large and small, will likely affect your practice every month.

The great wholesaler understands how to recover quickly, communicate with urgency, and make best efforts to turn negatives into positives.

How well do you recover?

Full, Few, or Two?

Oh, my aching back.

What started as the world's greatest mattress, one that found its place in the sleeping hall of fame, has betrayed me.

Today it's like sleeping on a cotton ball; I'm barely able to extricate myself from its torturous clutches in the morning.

So The Mrs. and I head to the mattress store to buy the latest promise of heavenly sleep, having done our homework before setting foot in the store.

At one point in the discussion, the salesman proudly exclaims that, "This mattress is covered by a full twenty-five-year warranty!"

BS detector fully engaged I ask, "But how long is it covered at one hundred percent?"

To which he quietly mumbles, "The first few years."

No small detail, as in this case "few" is actually two and "full" means partial—the coverage declines every year after two.

Great wholesalers aren't tempted to edit the facts and endanger the relationship, for the benefit of the sale.

It's Hard to Be Humble

"Oh Lord it's hard to be humble when you're perfect in every way." —Mac Davis

New suit?

Check.

Starched white shirt?

Check.

Dimpled tie knot?

Check.

Great group of advisors assembled with their manager for a fabulous lunch at a ritzy outdoor cafe on a bright, warm California summer day?

Check.

Ketchup bottle exploding upon opening all over new suit, starched white shirt, and dimpled tie?

Check.

Clearly the universe's reminder to take the job seriously but not myself.

———

"Stay humble, and stay hungry."
—*The Millionaire Wholesaler*

Sam I Am

I'm a bit delusional.

A few years ago, I thought about hiring a private jet for a vacation.

I came to my senses when I got my head around how much that would really cost.

At the time, I mistakenly gave my email address to the charter-jet company's sales rep, Sam.

Here's the email I get from him once every six months:

"I hope all is well. I am just checking in to see if you have any upcoming flights that you would like me to price out for you. You may reach me anytime via email or phone. Have a great day!"

Sam, Sam, Sam.

You are trying to appeal to a buyer [clearly not me] who thinks nothing of shelling out $30,000 for a round-trip flight in a G550, and that's the best you have?

Although it's not too far off from the questionable caliber of communications that wannabe wholesalers send.

Being able to craft actionable, compelling messaging, either written or verbal, never goes out of sales style.

And is a hallmark of a great wholesaler.

Who Brung You to the Dance?

Barry was an advisor in San Diego.

My internal and I courted him—hard.

We were relentless in our pursuit.

And then it happened.

[cue: the clouds parting, sun shining, heavenly angels singing]

Barry dropped his first ticket.

Then the second one.

And during the year he became a top producer.

Which, since I had a lesson to learn back then, meant that I stopped the courtship.

So Barry stopped producing.

In a painful call to win him back, he introduced me to a phrase I have not forgotten, "Dance with the one that brung you."

Which, translated, means, "How could I be so shortsighted as to take Barry's business for granted?"

Are you dancing with the ones that brung you?

———

**"Never, ever let a relationship
go to autopilot."**
—*The Millionaire Wholesaler*

Easy Rider

All hail the wholesaler.

The road warrior.

There's nothing we like better than open lanes of freshly paved highway—with speed limits at seventy-five miles per hour.

And as I experienced this week in the heartland, with nary a crack nor pothole to be found, the journey is both fast and efficient.

Unlike Los Angeles, or Tulsa, or New York City, which were recently ranked as among the major urban areas where poor roads cost drivers the most.

Kind of like the journey of your wholesaling practice.

Well maintained, your practice (the Process, the People, the PVP) hum right along.

Unattended, the journey gets a whole lot harder.

The road becomes rougher.

And starts to cost you money.

You are the driver of your region.

When was the last time you checked for potholes in your practice?

———

"It's important to constantly be a sponge in this business."
—The Millionaire Wholesaler

Just a Wholesaler

Three hours that go by in the blink of an eye.

That was the sensation I had last Saturday morning when I sat down for a discussion with Alan.

He is both a veteran of the financial services community and a member of the Speaker Hall of Fame.

And he related a story that deeply troubled me.

Seems a number of years ago, an advisor requested a speaker from management to attend a client function.

Unfortunately the manager was unavailable.

So, naturally, the suggestion was made for the advisor to use the more than qualified local wholesaler for the gig.

The advisor's reply?

"No, he's just the wholesaler."

Excuse me?

Just a wholesaler?

Sadly that wholesaler, in the eyes of the advisor, was already swallowed up by the Sea of Sameness.

What one thing will you do this week that makes it abundantly clear that you are not, nor will not ever be, just a wholesaler?

———

"I don't compare myself to the average wholesaler."
—*The Millionaire Wholesaler*

Relationship Glue

What if Bill knew me?

Not all of me, but just a part of me.

The easy part, that relates to my professional background.

For it wouldn't be hard for Bill to know me—I'm strewn all over the web.

In one simple search, he'd have seen—in almost an instant—that I no longer reside in Corporate America but make my home in Entrepreneurial America instead.

And, if he took that brief moment to know me, he would have saved himself precious time, effort, and the embarrassment of looking like another poorly informed, ill-prepared sales schlep who bobs along in the Great Sea of Sameness.

That's what I thought about Bill, who called and left a message to solicit his company's "new zip-code solution for asset management and insurance distributors" that today has zero relevance to my business.

Wholesalers, the relationship glue you seek may be only a click away.

How well do you prepare for the calls you make?

———

"Relevance is the ability to stay involved with advisors while helping them grow their businesses."
—*The Millionaire Wholesaler*

If You're Bored, I'm Bored

It started like any other wine tasting.

The Mrs. and I wheeled up to the winery, and we were met by a fresh-faced host who enthusiastically welcomed us.

After his brief explanation of the tasting options, Dave appeared from a side door.

Dave, not all fresh-faced, extolled his thirty-plus years of experience in The Valley and proceeded to monotonically put us to sleep with his description of the wines we sipped.

All the while he was practicing his golf swing with his imaginary five iron.

Good thing he's the Director of Visitor Relations.

You can't make this up.

Four wines into this stop, The Mrs. was shopping the one table with winery trinkets and trash—which is code for "get me the hell out of here."

"If you're bored, I'm bored," The Mrs. observed about Dave as we drove away.

And it reminded me of how great wholesalers are able to make every meeting, every day, enthusiastically seem like it's their fresh-faced debut.

The Untouchables

In 1959 it was a TV series with Robert Stack.

In 1987 it was a movie with Kevin Costner.

In your practice for 2014, *The Untouchables* are those advisors that you covet.

The Elephants that will change your world—but won't take your call.

Just thinking about a meeting with *The Untouchables* makes you giddy and nervous, at the same time.

Know this about *The Untouchables*:

1. You can't lead with only product.

2. You need a clear idea of what your PVP—Peerless Value Proposition® is.

3. You will need to be innovative in your marketing approach.

As you think about your plan for the year ahead, how will you memorably and systematically attack *The Untouchables* in your territory?

Thirty-Five Ways to Kill It in the Year Ahead

Hindsight is twenty-twenty.

Looking back at your almost complete year, was it your Career Year?

Based on the eight-hundred-plus hours of coaching we have done with our wholesaler and management clients this past year, here's a partial list of thirty-five ways to ensure that next year exceeds your expectations:

- Commit to writing a good business plan.
- Commit to looking at your business plan after it is written.
- Formulate rotations that are well informed by the data.
- Stick to the rotations you built.
- Learn to say no more effectively.
- Create and market your PVP—Peerless Value Proposition®.
- Write emails that get opened, read, and acted upon.
- Perfect the "come to Jesus" conversation, so you don't get monetarily taken advantage of.
- Deepen the relationship you have with your internal wholesaler.

- Find ways to outsource things that you shouldn't be spending time on.
- Stay current on your expenses.
- Automate and be diligent with your call report notes.
- Have a system to say thank you to the advisors who "brought you to the dance."
- Never neglect your COIs.
- Use technology frequently and creatively.
- Make the best use of LinkedIn that you possibly can.
- Use premeeting agendas.
- Do your advisor intelligence before appointments.
- Stop dwelling on daily sales, and focus on the right activity.
- Don't confuse activity with results.
- Make forward scheduling a habit.
- Admit when you need assistance.
- Develop better listening skills.
- Become a well-informed student of the business.
- Define and implement repeatable processes for your practice.
- Seek out improvements in your presentation skills.
- Know what is, and isn't, worth falling on your sword for.
- Challenge convention.
- Liberally exercise your creative brain.
- Explore ways to make the job fun [again].
- Be home when you are home.
- Keep your financial house in order.

- Take time off to recharge.
- Be a leader among your peers.
- Know that old dogs can learn new tricks.

We Hit the Lottery

I'm a sucker for games of chance.

So when the local market offers an entry to a drawing for a weekly gift certificate, you know I'm in.

The rules are simple: be green and bring your own bag, get a ticket, match the ticket numbers posted weekly to win.

Bright and early New Year's Day, I head off for the market for coffee and to check the numbers with the same delusional optimism that precedes every chance to win.

Of the six numbers on my ticket, I had five...and the last number was off by one.

As I slunk away and contemplated what might have been of a one-hundred-dollar bounty, I quickly remembered this:

The fact that we have the chance to work in this profession, with the folks that we do, to make the money that we make, and afford the things that we have is hitting the lottery.

The first full week of your Career Year starts now.

Go cash in big-time.

Wholesaler Cocoon of Complacency

The phrase leapt out of my mouth in conversation with my coach (yes, coaches have coaches too).

It captures the state of being that, if we aren't careful, we find ourselves in—seemingly by surprise.

It's where competency bleeds into laziness.

It's the often false sense of security that envelops us when we have been wholesaling long enough.

Long enough to know how to do it.

And long enough to stop asking why or how we do what we do.

It's a fragile, cozy, warm covering that can be punctured easily by our competition.

An isolated place that insulates us from getting to our goals.

The cocoon of complacency.

A fine place to be if you are a centipede.

A dangerous place to live as a wholesaler.

———

**"Never be too comfortable,
satisfied or complacent."**
—*The Millionaire Wholesaler*

Just Be Better

Work out more.

Lose weight.

Spend more time home when I'm home.

Every January, friends, family, and colleagues want to know about our New Year's resolutions.

As a culture we seem to obsess about the many ways in which we might transform our lives from where they were on December 31 to where they should be in the year ahead.

Blame Janus.

He is the mythical Roman King Janus, for whom January was named.

With two faces, one looking ahead and one looking at the past, Janus became the symbol for resolutions back "in the day"—153 BC.

According to *Psychology Today*, the two most popular resolutions are to quit smoking and decrease consumption of alcohol.

And, not surprisingly, 60 percent have failed in their efforts after only six months.

Here's an alternative approach: how about if we simply start the year by choosing to be better?

Be a better wholesaler, be a better manager, be a better parent, be a better friend—just be better.

Yes, the naysayers will offer that this is too vague of a goal.

And they might be right.

And they also might be part of the 60 percent who fail.

Rearview Mirror Test

Nothing good happens in my rearview mirror.

In fact, the rearview mirror has been the location of some of the most humbling conversations I've ever had—with myself.

And I'll bet you've been there too.

Like the complete waste of a prospect who causes you to get in the car after the appointment, look in the rearview mirror, and exclaim out loud, "Why did I agree to see that jerk?"

Or the meeting that started with all kinds of promise and then slipped away because you got off track.

Which inspires you to get in the car, look in the rearview mirror, and say, "What just happened in there?"

Today I introduce you to a new test for wholesaler self-improvement—the Rearview Mirror Test.

Simply catalog the conversations you have with yourself in the rearview mirror over the course of the next thirty days by category.

If you're like me, it'll be a good starting point to iden-tify your areas of improvement on the road to your next Career Year.

"The rearview mirror is always clearer than the wind-shield."—Warren Buffett

Half-Pregnant Wholesaling?

Half-pregnant.

An expression that symbolizes a lack of commitment.

After all, there is no such thing.

This week I had the honor of speaking to a team of top-flight wholesalers in Toronto.

On the way back to the airport, I commented to the limo driver about the extraordinary explosion of condos erupting on the city's skyline.

After telling me a story about a pal who was getting financially soaked in the hype of allegedly rising real estate prices, he said something that caught my ear.

"I'm a part-time mortgage broker," he explained. "That's how I know about this market."

His comment stopped me in my tracks.

Here it is, 12:30 p.m. on a Tuesday afternoon and you're driving a limo—not working at your mortgage broker practice during prime business hours, I thought.

What would happen if he went all in?

If he dedicated 100 percent of his efforts to being an all-star mortgage broker or a best-in-class limo driver.

Are you all in with your wholesaling practice?

Or is your territory half-pregnant?

———

"I control my effort and my attitude and make sure that both are better than everybody else's."
—*The Millionaire Wholesaler*

I'll Take the Ginsu Knives

It's a love/hate thing.

Infomercials.

Generally seen as I awake only half coherent at 2:00 a.m. to turn off the TV.

Raise your hand if you remember the Popeil Pocket Fisherman or ShamWow.

And who hasn't seen the ads for P90X?

As much as late-night infomercials grate on our nerves, there are valuable lessons to be learned from them for great wholesalers.

Arguably the best lesson is one of scarcity.

You've heard the pitch: "our Make Your First Billion Dollars in Foreclosed Real Estate seminar is only open to the first three hundred people who respond to the sound of my voice," says the voice over announcer.

As a wholesaler, one of the ways to increase your value, and the value of your best ideas and information, is by making them scarcer.

Does everyone in your region get all you have to offer?

Have you created well-defined service models?

Do you need help figuring out how to properly position scarcity?

Wholesaling Cronuts®

It's a doughnut.

It's a croissant.

It's a five-dollar pastry that attracts so much attention that the very name has been trademarked.

So many people line up to indulge in this sinful delight that their website offers proper protocols of line etiquette, complete with a statement that says, "we hope you don't endorse any scalpers you may see."

For a pastry!

There are approximately six thousand retail bakeries in the United States.

Yet Dominique Ansel Bakery has brilliantly executed the art of exclusivity in a most unlikely place.

Which leads us to you and your practice.

What do you have besides product and service (both wholesaling table stakes) that advisors might line up to get a taste of?

Have you baked an offering that opens doors and allows you to market in a way that separates you from the vast Sea of Sameness?

What are you doing to create and market your PVP—Peerless Value Proposition®?

———

"If I differentiate myself from everyone else, I'm in the game."
—*The Millionaire Wholesaler*

Stop the Insanity

Screaming down the 405 freeway.

Eighteen minutes to get to an appointment that takes twenty minutes to reach.

Voice mail says there are twelve unheard messages.

Last check of email indicates thirty-seven unread messages.

The next trip to Northern California isn't even booked yet.

A seminar tonight for which materials have yet to arrive.

And next week's schedule is more open than full.

Sound familiar?

The constant endless stream of business thoughts/tasks cascading through your head.

Unlike the nine-to-five worker, our lifestyles (a.k.a. jobs) have this built-in hazard.

And, if you're not careful, the thoughts will overtake you.

And run you over.

Unless you take time.

Time to stop.

Time to listen.

Time to just be.

———

**"Spend more quiet time to think about
what you need to achieve."**
—*The Millionaire Wholesaler*

By the Length of an Outstretched Toe

Good-bye, Sochi.

It was a fun, if long, two weeks.

And, as the highlight reels of gold, silver, and bronze make their last appearances, I couldn't help but notice a phenomenon.

The stretch.

Or the lunge.

You've seen it.

Biathletes crossing the finish line extending the toe of their ski.

Speed skaters attempting to get the very tip of their skate across the line milliseconds ahead of the next skater.

The world of wholesaling, one in which products are more similar than not, is often decided by the smallest of margins as well.

The way in which you engage in our "sport" will determine your position.

A nameless face in the great Sea of Sameness.

Or a position on the medals podium—one of the truly great wholesalers.

And, in 2014, that margin will likely be decided by a nose.

Which begs the question: how far are you stretching?

Old Habits Die Hard

The month closed on the twenty-fifth.

The goal was to get to at least $30,000 gross.

There it was the twentieth, and it was a stretch to think $15,000 was doable.

And as much as I tried to keep that production anxiety in check, when I saw my next client I knew he could tell.

It was a vibe they could sense.

A "damn this is a terrible month, and I really need you to buy, but I'm doing my best not to show it" vibe.

Later as a new wholesaler, the numbers (daily, weekly, monthly) became the obsession.

Old habits die hard you know.

Finally the light bulb went on.

The one that I knew to be true but fought hard to accept.

The one that says we can control only what we can control.

Activity and attitude.

Repeat after me, "Activity and attitude, activity and attitude, activity and attitude."

———

"Have a positive attitude every day."
—*The Millionaire Wholesaler*

Obvious Allies and Overlooked Advocates

He was entitled to his opinion.

It happened at dinner the night before the workshop I was conducting.

Sitting across the table from me was a long-tenured wholesaler.

"What's your attitude about centers of influence?" he asked. "I don't pay any attention to them because all they want is money."

And over the next fifteen minutes, he found a way to dispel any truth that has ever been offered or known about the power of solid COI relationships.

He intentionally chose to overlook advocates and shun obvious allies.

Maybe his approach was all wrong.

Maybe he really had nothing to offer COIs.

What's your strategy for centers of influence?

How, in this week ahead, can you improve this part of your practice?

———

"Work smart and try to see the influential people in the office."

—*The Millionaire Wholesaler*

Million-Mile Flyer

It was worn like a badge of honor.

And the flight that put me over the top was downright celebratory.

Never again would qualification for status be needed at United Airlines.

And so it was with Hilton and Hertz and…well you get the idea.

Loyalty programs are wonderfully hideous.

Wonderful because of the perceived value.

Hideous because of the lengths we'll go to just to stay loyal.

Like flying from Chicago to Los Angeles, with a stopover in Newark, because they have a promotion for double miles.

Not that that's ever happened…

While perks directly correlated to business in our world are ill advised and flagrant infractions for most, service levels—the first cousin of loyalty programs—are another story.

How do you segment the "what you have to offer" and "who you offer it to"?

Do all advisors get all your best stuff (think seminars, marketing support, and business building assistance), or do you have identifiable tiers of service?

How do you best craft and describe these service levels?

Quiet on the Set!

Bored.

Disengaged.

Too many meetings we attend leave us feeling this way.

Which is why I was always committed to one meeting per year that would keep my team buzzing for months, if not years, after the event.

One year I relented and approved a meeting in Las Vegas— as I had always contended that Las Vegas and productive meetings were not synonymous.

The main event was a full-day affair wherein we provided each team of seven a video camera, a driver, and a cooler full of beverages and told them to shoot their own commercial for Las Vegas.

We then sent them to an editing studio for final touches.

And, just to raise the stakes, we had members of the Las Vegas Convention and Visitors Authority on-site the following day to judge the final versions.

While I am sworn to secrecy regarding the actual content of said videos (the whole "stays in Vegas" thing), I assure you that the event was memorable indeed.

How about your events with advisors?

How creative is your approach?

How memorable are your events?

The Weight of Your Bag

That hard-sided Samsonite briefcase wasn't going to cut it.

Not if I wanted to be taken seriously as a wholesaler.

And, while shelling out over $350 for the first Tumi bag gave me heart palpitations, I now looked the part.

I filled that bag with a four-inch-thick war book, sales ideas, notebook, assorted consumer brochures, and an assortment of pens, highlighters, and the like.

After managing to zip the bag closed, I estimated that it weighed an easy twenty-five pounds.

I am also reasonably sure it aided and abetted a slip disk.

As the years progressed, the weight of the bag lightened, seemingly coinciding with the ability to streamline processes, delegate tasks, and absorb more knowledge.

Is the bag on your shoulder starting to ache?

What do you need to do to lighten the weight of your bag?

———

"Systematize your life."
—The Millionaire Wholesaler

Chicken and Waffles

Chicken and waffles?

An absurd idea.

That is until 1975 when Herb Hudson opened a now-famous restaurant in Los Angeles called Roscoe's.

He had the crazy idea of mixing chicken and waffles.

On the same plate!

Now, forty years later, chicken and waffles is a staple at so many great restaurants.

So what's this got to do with wholesaling?

Plenty, when you consider how many wholesalers are unwilling or incapable of exploring new and creative ideas.

Ideas that will enhance your MQ—Memorability Quotient®—in the minds of clients and prospects.

After all, if the advisor doesn't remember the content of your last visit or call, it might as well have never happened.

"I can't understand why people are frightened of new ideas. I'm frightened of the old ones." —John Cage

This week, why not try out a new idea that is truly different and memorable?

The Trunk Show

The bolts were carefully arranged in a pristine display case.

The fabrics displayed were made of only the highest quality cotton, wool, linen, and silk.

Every sales person was in maximum suck up mode, hoping a new custom suit order, or five, would be theirs.

They escorted clients to tailors who meticulously tucked, pinned, and marked each inch of fabric to be altered to ensure the best possible fit.

After multiple return visits to refine the perfect fit and to acquire all of the accompanying accessories, the quintessential wholesaler wardrobe was complete.

And then in the very first meeting, wrapped in the confidence of the highest quality blends of cotton, wool, linen, and silk, the wholesaler had the moment that strikes us all—but is left unspoken.

"What if I'm just another suit, in another office, carrying another briefcase?"

The most insidious villain in your territory might be the one that lives between your two ears.

———

"Your behavior, attitude and your approach can make all the difference exponentially over time."
—*The Millionaire Wholesaler*

It's About Time

The Kromega III.

A watch so complex it takes two people to make it work.

That was a *Saturday Night Live* commercial spoof circa 1977.

Fast-forward to last week's announcement that we now have a clock that is the world's most accurate.

In fact, the NIST-F2 is accurate to within one second in 300 million years.

Which is important news, as it is precise timekeeping that underpins our modern world and your practice.

GPS, for instance, needs an accuracy of about a billionth of a second to keep you from getting lost in route to seeing your next advisor.

Great wholesalers know that part of their greatness is the precision with which they run their day.

Always on time and within time.

Such a seemingly simple nuance—that so many find so difficult.

———

"Be honest, be on time and wrap it up in an appropriate time frame."
—*The Millionaire Wholesaler*

A Valuable Lesson Learned

She was one of the firm's most tenured wholesalers.

A top-three producer.

She had been in that position for years.

Unfortunately, she also had public opinions about everything.

And made those opinions known to any and all within earshot.

Including senior management at national meetings.

During one national sales meeting session, she reached a tipping point, voicing her audible displeasure to anyone and everyone.

The last we saw of her was as she exited a conference room, moments before the national sales manager and CEO exited.

And she did not reappear.

The lesson learned?

Super wholesaling success affords you a voice.

Use that voice unwisely and you risk bankrupting your career.

Beatnik Art

Some mistake it for a winery.

A seemingly simply property off of Highway 12 between Napa and Sonoma.

Upon further inspection you realize it's not a winery at all but an art museum.

A two-hundred-plus acre property founded by Rene di Rosa, who started his career as a reporter for the *San Francisco Chronicle* in 1950.

He lived within the San Francisco beatnik art community where he developed a passion for the works of emerging Bay Area artists.

Yet the word passion, as I observed it while touring his legacy, just didn't adequately describe his level of love for the two-thousand-plus pieces on display.

He had devotion, intensity, and a dedication to his pursuit that was so clear I could feel it as I walked the grounds.

Which got me thinking about you.

And your practice.

And the passion that you have, or don't, for the work that you do.

Because to your advisors passion is palpable.

True Confessions

Guilty as charged.

Work consumes who I am.

It defines my existence.

And I am not proud of this fact.

And I'm damn sure not alone.

You get paid a ton of money relative to other professions, and you work endlessly.

How many family and/or life events have you missed?

One time I was away for my wife's birthday, and my boss called to apologize to her that his meeting conflicted with her celebration.

As a coach, I hear about breakups, divorces, missed kids' soccer matches, missed parent-teacher conferences, etc.

The reality is some of this comes with the turf—it's part of the price you pay.

But can you add more balance to your work-life equation?

———

"Don't put all your eggs in your business basket; you're going to burn out. Have a life too."

—The Millionaire Wholesaler

Wholesaler Trust Premium

All bids were for the same job.

Contractor #1 bids $10,000.

Contractor #2 bids $11,000.

Contractor #3 bids $11,800.

Being the ever thrifty homeowner, I am drawn to the lowest bid.

Then again, the "experts" say the middle bid is the one that should be selected.

But what about if you had previous experience with contractor #3, the high bidder?

And that prior experience proved to be positive.

There was clear communication; both buyer and seller knew what to expect.

The work was done on time, and there were no surprises.

Ultimately you trusted both their word and their work.

Perhaps those attributes of the first experience may well be worth the 18 percent premium in price.

Similarly, your return is not currently top decile.

Your rate presently is off by fifteen basis points.

Your rider was repriced with twenty basis points less of a guarantee.

And yet, the great wholesaler continues to outperform.

What's your trust premium?

———

"Getting the trust factor so that the advisors will call you is a core part of the process."
—*The Millionaire Wholesaler*

Your Big Ego

"Where ego I go too."

So read a button that a former coworker gave to me, only partially in jest.

And for a wholesaler, ego is as much a defense shield as it is a necessary part of his or her DNA.

But left unchecked, our ego makes us do things we know better not to do.

Such as insisting that the ninth time we visit an advisor will magically be the one that triggers his or her first ticket.

It's our ego that says, "I know I'll win them over!"

Or, mistakenly, dialing up the cockiness as the annual income increases.

It's our ego that gets intoxicated and out of control.

Great wholesalers have a handle on their ego—and use it to play both offense and defense in a winning way.

———

> **"One of the greatest mistakes a wholesaler makes is thinking that they're better than their client."**
> —*The Millionaire Wholesaler*

The Sleazy Close

It was going to be an easy sale.

Hell, it was his to lose.

The dealership was owned by the family of a friend.

Knowing that my wholesaling mobile, the 1988 Nissan Maxima, was in need of an upgrade, I identified the new model I wanted and headed to the car lot.

As soon as I sat down at the salesperson's desk and told him of my interest in the car, he slid a blank piece of paper and a pen across the desk and instructed me to write how much I wanted to pay for the car.

No discussion, no rapport building, and not even a handshake.

My response was to get up and leave.

It was, singularly, the most off-putting close I have ever experienced.

And so it is with the notion of closing for so many whole-salers, negatively influenced by sleazy behavior that they themselves have experienced.

Yet the great wholesaler knows how to move the sales process forward, to gain commitments, and do so without feeling like they need a shower after the appointment.

———

"Don't make the mistake of being too product focused."

—The Millionaire Wholesaler

And Then You Hit the Dip

Flying high.

There is no better feeling, is there?

You had a great month, landed the elusive client, and accomplished one of your major annual goals.

And, sure as heat comes in summer, there will be a time.

A time where your resolve is tested.

Your motivation wanes.

You hit the dip, you'll feel stuck, and you lose significant altitude relative to the heights at which you were flying.

It's happened to all of us before.

It will happen again.

The thing that separates the very best from the rest is the ability to power through.

———

"Don't ever quit, don't allow yourself to get discouraged."
—*The Millionaire Wholesaler*

The Lesson of Gary Chain

He was the CFO of a bank.

And the object of the search.

Gary Chain was the most highly compensated executive whom I ever placed, so many years ago as an executive recruiter.

The commission earned was sizable, and it began the syndrome that follows me to this day.

The same syndrome that likely follows you too.

It's the behavior we fall into when we get a big ticket.

Which rolls up to a great month.

Which leads to statements, when congratulated about that month, such as, "Oh, but I had a big trade."

Somehow feeling like we need to discount the fact that we earned the business.

Yet, such statements infer it may have been a fluke or that we were not deserving.

Raise your right hand and repeat after me, "I will revel in the fact that I got a huge deal, and I will not downplay it."

The sales gods giveth, and they taketh away.

Let's revel when they giveth.

Everything Is Urgent

The call came from the New York home office.

"Rob, we'd like for an exec from our ad agency to ride with you," said the head of marketing.

Never one to turn down a guest who wanted to know more about our craft, I eagerly agreed.

Once we were in the car and freeway bound, the exec's pager [yes, pager] began to go off.

Repeatedly.

Aside from a brief glance to discern who was paging him, the exec took no action.

After about the fifth time this occurred, I couldn't help but ask, "Don't you need to respond to your page?"

To which he replied with a wry smile, "Everything is urgent; therefore, nothing is urgent."

If that was true twenty years ago, how much truth is there to it in today's connected world?

Today you need to be discerning with your time and manage it well.

Maintaining a high degree of urgency while knowing that not everything is urgent.

———

"Returning advisor calls is always an urgent matter."

—*The Millionaire Wholesaler*

Sorry, You've Been Chopped

True confession: cooking shows are my vice.

Top Chef, Chopped, MasterChef—I TiVo them all.

Somewhere in my delusional mind, the fantasy of being able to create a Michelin three-star meal rattles around—as if it will ever be achieved simply by watching one of these shows.

This past week I attended the premier educational conference for professional speakers, and among the many terrific quotes I captured, this one resonated:

"A list of ingredients doesn't make you a chef." —Jay Baer

In our craft this translates to the following: just because you have a stack of product information in your bag, know that your firm has good value add programs, employ a scheduler, partner with an internal, and possess an expense account, these do not make you a great wholesaler.

Great wholesalers don't simply have the list of ingredients.

They know how to masterfully blend the ingredients to create a practice that gets rave critical acclaim.

How about you and your practice?

Are you working on your Michelin star—or are you close to getting chopped?

———

"My scheduler is as much a key as my internal wholesaler."
—*The Millionaire Wholesaler*

The Irrelevant Wholesaler

Oh, the "good old days."

He remembers fondly stopping by the side of the road and making calls from pay phones.

She reminisces about handwritten call reports.

He longs for the return of the steak-and-whiskey days.

The problem starts when he disclaims, "I'm not real good with a smartphone or iPad."

Or she proudly pronounces that using the firm's multimillion-dollar CRM isn't something she intends to embrace.

Perhaps there was a time, in the "good old days," when your boss would look the other way—because you were a top producer.

But today, in an era when stock trades happen in milliseconds, there isn't the same latitude afforded.

The competition is too fierce; the speed of business too great.

Wholesalers who refuse to embrace the way things are and only pine for the way things were are about as relevant to a firm as hand-crank pencil sharpeners and mimeograph machines.

————

"Great wholesalers understand how to use technology both for organization and for productivity."
—The Millionaire Wholesaler

Don't Tell Me What to Do

Stubborn.

It's my way or the highway.

And for the love of all that is holy, don't tell me what to do.

That said, consider that there are way too many choices in this world.

Last time I went to Target, I got tooth decay just standing there trying to decide which of the 113 flavor and size varieties of Crest toothpaste I should buy.

In the soup aisle, I burned calories reading through the thirty-plus flavors of Campbell's soup (and all seventy-four available were not on display).

Your advisors see more than a few wholesalers, and generally each one offers many choices.

They offer multiple riders, share classes, death benefits, plan limits, and so forth.

Is it any wonder the advisor might be paralyzed by choice?

What if you were the one wholesaler who told the advisor, based on your savvy analysis of their circumstance, specifically what they should sell?

And then showed them exactly how to sell it.

You Gotta Believe

What was I thinking?

Recently I assumed that I could man up and haul tons of old cinder blocks out of the backyard.

Sadly, this feat only served to reaggravate a herniated disk injury from twenty years ago—with a vengeance.

Determined not to undergo surgery, I sought out alternative options.

Enter Diana.

She's a seventy-plus-year-old practitioner of a little-known form of massage.

No, not the "I think it would be lovely to have a massage at the spa at the Ritz" variety.

She seeks to heal by, for example, spending twenty minutes making certain the energy in your left earlobe is correct.

Or realigning the body in crevices that are normally reserved for your significant other.

To be clear, I am a cynical pragmatist and a traditionalist, especially when it comes to my health.

But in this case I decided to believe.

Now, eight sessions later, and mostly pain-free, I'm glad I did.

In your practice you have to make decisions to believe every week.

To set any cynicism and doubt aside.

To trust that if you take care of the numbers, the numbers will take care of you.

And, most importantly, you gotta believe in yourself.

The Thinker

The president of the distributor had an announcement to make.

"I've decided to reorganize and add another layer of management to our growing firm. In doing so I'll have more time to think."

To which I distinctly remember thinking, "I'm busting my hump in the field every day, barely able to breathe, and you'll have more time to *think*?"

Only later did I understand the significance of what he was saying.

He, and you, need time to think.

To reflect.

To assess.

To evaluate.

To process.

To plan.

To ideate.

To stew, mull, marinate, or just plain be at peace with your thoughts.

You are in a marathon profession.

Stop running your practice like it's a sprint.

———

"Every year is a marathon and too many wholesalers get burned out because they don't have balance."
—*The Millionaire Wholesaler*

Every Customer Is a Good Customer

Chicken farmers are up in arms.

Courtesy of Mr. Putin.

Seems Pooty-Poot (thanks to Dubya for that name) has placed an embargo on EU and US food imports.

Rest assured I'm not venturing where I don't belong, offering economic commentary, but I did hear a snippet this week that made me blanch.

"Every customer is a good customer," said the chicken farmer, lamenting the loss of Russian consumers.

Which may be true if you are selling poultry.

But in the sale of financial products to financial advisors, every client is most certainly not a good client.

In fact, there are clients you need to run (not walk) from as fast as your dress-shoed feet will take you.

The overpromisers and underdelivers need to be culled from your book.

As do the "what's yours is mine, and what's mine is mine" abusers who think nothing of sucking your budget, and your energy, bone-dry.

Your job is too demanding to spread your considerable talents too lovingly on those folks who have no appreciation, and sometimes outright disdain, for what you do.

Feel free to quietly, not publicly, fire these advisors.

After all, you have better fish (or chicken) to fry.

Front Row Center

Billy Joel and Elton John.

Two artists who contributed to the soundtrack of my life.

So in 2001, when they performed in San Diego, I knew I had to be there.

But the show was sold out, and tickets were expensive in the secondary market.

Being thrifty as I am (The Mrs. says "cheap"), I was going to opt for lesser-priced tickets.

To which The Mrs. replied, "If you're passionate about their music, spend the money."

Advice well heeded—we sat front row center.

Recently, I spoke with a Millionaire Wholesaler interviewee who sits front row center.

In fact, he called himself a "Front Row Guy."

He sits up front in meetings.

He makes sure he doesn't miss any information.

He prides himself on being a sponge, learning constantly.

How about you?

Are you passionately seated in the front row of your practice?

———

"One habit that is ingrained in me is that every single day I'm committed."

—*The Millionaire Wholesaler*

Lofty Advisor Expectations

He was an ascending top producer.

I was a new(er) wholesaler.

Each time I saw him, he shared his grand scheme for a client event to top all client events.

On one visit he took me up to the Oriental Suite on the forty-eighth floor of the Mandarin Oriental Hotel in San Francisco.

He stood on the two-thousand-square-foot balcony and waved his arms in one direction (the Golden Gate Bridge) and then another (the Bay Bridge), speaking about the catering and the jazz combo and where the bar would be placed.

At this point I was sweating bullets, since my budget was tighter than a sumo wrestler in a pair of skinny jeans.

How would I tell him his plan was too grand?

Should I have even agreed to see the suite where he envisioned the event?

What youth hostel would I be staying in for the rest of my wholesaling career—since this event would eat up my entire budget?

Soon after the advisor moved offices, to the suburbs.

Budget and potential relationship crisis averted.

And lesson learned: saying no too early can unnecessarily damage the relationship.

Sometimes we need to see where lofty expectations lead.

––––––

"Manage expectations."

—The Millionaire Wholesaler

The Curious Wholesaler

Smart folks.

We work in a sector that is filled with supersmart folks.

Many have IQs worthy of Mensa consideration.

And, if we're lucky, those same brilliant minds have an EQ—Emotional Quotient—that is as developed as their IQ is.

Yet after reading a piece in the *Harvard Business Review* recently, I'm convinced that the greatest wholesalers are also gifted with a terrifically high CQ.

The author, Dr. Tomas Chamorro-Premuzic, explains:

"CQ stands for curiosity quotient and concerns having a hungry mind. People with higher CQ are more inquisitive and open to new experiences. They find novelty exciting and are quickly bored with routine. They tend to generate many original ideas and are counterconformist."

It follows, then, that high IQ plus high EQ plus high CQ equals a high MQ.

What's your MQ—Memorability Quotient®?

———

"You're not going to win every battle, and that's OK."

—The Millionaire Wholesaler

Shine Artist

Simple moments of wholesaling pleasure.

Tucked away in the far corner of Nordstrom, there was a shoeshine stand.

For five dollars, including tip, you could get a mighty fine shine from Connie, who took her job seriously indeed.

If you happen to be in Chicago and run into Stan, as I did in 2012, you'll meet a man who is equally hardworking and dedicated.

At that time he said, reflecting on his sense of family obligation, "I don't care; I'll drywall, lay tile, or shine shoes."

"I'll find a way to make a living while my friends sit at home jobless and complain about child support," he said.

"My dad always told me that ones is better than nones."

He too offered a really great shine.

But as hard as Connie and Stan worked, it pales in comparison with Leon.

Leon Frisby to be precise.

Whose sign I saw this week, next to his busy stand in the hotel lobby, which read:

Leon Frisby
Shine Artist

Leon has a brand.

Do you?

What's your PVP—Peerless Value Proposition®?

Aptitude, Attitude, Altitude

The dreaded first interview.

You can tell a lot about the future success of a wholesaler during that first interview.

Especially when applicants are asked to "describe yourself using one-word adjectives."

Or "what's the most difficult decision you ever had to make?"

Recently I had a chance to visit with aspiring young professionals at the nonprofit Year Up.

Year Up's mission is, "to close the Opportunity Divide by providing urban young adults with the skills, experience, and support that will empower them to reach their potential through professional careers and higher education."

To get accepted, the rigorous interview includes screening for the aptitude elements you might expect, and two attitude screens that resonated:

- Grit
- Resilience

Year Up knows that making a move from the streets of the inner city to the payrolls of some of the greatest companies in America doesn't happen without both qualities.

Not unlike truly great wholesalers—those who possess courage and resolve (grit) plus the toughness required to recover quickly from difficulties (resilience).

"I control my effort and my attitude and make sure that both are better than everybody else's."

—The Millionaire Wholesaler

Pay Yourself First

An artist in concrete.

Best in the county.

These are but two of the accolades heaped on Darrell the Concrete Guy.

So busy was Darrell's crew that we waited an extra three weeks, into what was to be a thirty-day project, just to secure his services.

Oh, and his work was good.

Which can't be said about his finances.

Darrell had a nasty habit of sending his invoice for services at 8:00 p.m. via email and then texting at 6:00 a.m. the following morning to see if he could "swing by and pick up a check to meet payroll."

Even though he was busier than a long-tailed cat in a room full of rocking chairs, he didn't have his finances in order.

Not unlike too many wholesalers—some of whom I'll bet you know.

They make money hand over fist.

And spend it just as fast.

Our interviews with *The Millionaire Wholesaler* remind us that the next correction, reorg, layoff, and basis-point adjustment is just around bend.

Which is why financially secure wholesalers pay themselves first.

———

"Living within your means today is a path to great wealth tomorrow."

—The Millionaire Wholesaler

The Digital Wholesaling Divide

Los Angeles Times.

Wall Street Journal.

New York Times.

At one point some years ago, each of these publications was delivered to my home daily.

By the end of the week, it was hard to see my desk amid the stack of newsprint.

Today all of that content sits on a 9.4 inch × 6.67 inch digital device.

Which is nothing short of miraculous.

And, truth be told, I sometimes need to touch a real newspaper.

There's just something about turning the pages and getting the counter smudged with newsprint, which is not replaced by a digital device.

And that's how advisors feel about the wholesaler who only presents in her style, without regard to how the advisor learns and absorbs information best.

You dutifully use your iPad to make all of your one-on-one presentations, and the advisors may long for being handed a brochure.

How do your advisors learn best?

What are you doing to accommodate their different learning styles?

————

"Have to be able to adapt to the new ways of communicating with advisors."
—*The Millionaire Wholesaler*

A Wholesaler in the Making?

The eighty eyeballs were laser focused.

They were there to extract as much information as they could from me in a short sixty minutes.

Each audience member—all eighteen to twenty-four years old—came prepared with remarkably insightful questions.

And while each person, based on the questions, had done some research, Jonathan had clearly done his homework best.

He knew the release date of our Wholesaler Masterminds® app, quoted concepts from *Brotherhood of the Bag: A Wholesaler's Handbook*, and cited various factoids about my background.

He asked questions that seemed more likely to come from an insider in our company and not a fresh-faced nineteen-year-old preparing to embark on his career.

Jonathan knew how to do thorough digital recon work and put that information to great use in his quest to learn.

The same recon work that great wholesalers perform on their advisors.

For the wholesaler who can connect to the advisors' intellect and emotion, their head and their heart, will find less resistance and form more meaningful relationships, more quickly.

How successfully do you incorporate advisor recon work into your process?

———

"Preparation is really a key ingredient to any success I've had."
—*The Millionaire Wholesaler*

The Disappearing Advisor

Sunny and seventy-two degrees.

Just another day in Southern California.

Appointment number three for the day was a bank advisor in Poway.

I settled into his guest chair and made the obligatory small talk, as I pulled my war book out of my bag.

Just as I transitioned into my best pitch on our Strategic Income Fund, an unforgettable site unfolded before me.

The advisor was slowly slipping down from his chair and gingerly making his way under the desk.

While at the same time silently mouthing to me, "Get on the floor."

A nanosecond later I heard a far more certain interpretation of that directive being screamed at everyone in the branch, as three masked and armed men jumped the teller counter.

While it felt like the better part of a week that I lay on the floor, contemplating the balance of my life and the triple shot of something that would be required to calm my nerves, in less than four minutes, it was over.

Oddly, the advisor and I reclaimed our original seats and closed the meeting in a far more organized fashion than you'd expect after the incident—and before the police arrived.

The stories we collect in our business are outrageous, unbelievable, disastrous, and comical—often at the same time!

Wholesaler Struck by Lightning

Have you been hit?

The VA that has the best-positioned rider on the street.

The Morningstar Gold, Five Star, and Lipper Leader fund that kills the competition.

The REIT that is closing in thirty days, and money is pouring in.

Most wholesalers have been there at least once.

And that's easy money.

But more often you are wholesaling through the assorted ups and downs of market and product cycles.

It's during that time, you need to

- Innovate;
- take risks;
- see one more advisor;
- tune up your marketing;
- make the extra phone call;
- get out of your comfort zone;

- nurture the relationship you have or wish to have with COIs; and
- put your PVP—Peerless Value Proposition®—on full display

If you are fortunate, that lightning will strike again.

"In order to get struck by lightning, you have to stand in the rain."—Joan Rivers, A Piece of Work

Ode to Tilly Butler

Her physical presence was humble.

Tilly's face had the weathered lines of a woman who had seen a lot of life's challenges.

As I made the product presentation, she displayed very little emotion to read.

It was impossible to know if I was even on the right sales track.

After pummeling her with features and benefits, I teed up a horribly feeble close.

To which she replied, "OK."

That was sale number one as an advisor some thirty years ago—and long before the wholesaling career.

And it provided a huge lesson.

You see, I never bothered to follow up with Tilly.

I foolishly assumed she was a woman of modest means.

Six months after my first sale to Tilly, a confirmation mistakenly landed on my desk.

It showed a mutual fund trade of $5,000,000.

A trade that was placed by another broker at my broker dealer—at a branch across town.

It turned out Tilly was loaded.

It also turned out that my client and prospect follow-up processes were nonexistent, which cost me plenty.

How about you?

How well have you bolted down your follow-up process?

Sea of Sameness Wholesaling

It's a dog-eat-dog career.

Your best client is the next wholesaler's best prospect.

Your firm's most innovative product concept is your competitor's new product launch in the blink of an eye.

The safety and security you feel, based on your long tenure, is like a crisp, clear pool of water that appears in the hot sand—an illusion.

Lately we learn of wholesalers who are being rightsized.

Downsized.

Dechannelized.

Rechannelized.

So what's your best defense?

Put down this email and go look in the mirror.

Ask yourself, and be as brutally honest as you can be, if you are simply going through the wholesaling motions.

Are you allowing yourself to slowly wade into the deep, dark, cold expanse that is the Sea of Sameness?

Or are you reinventing your processes.

Rethinking your approaches.

Reimagining your possibilities.

———

**"When you've achieved a high level
of success, the greatest danger is
maintaining the commitment and drive
to stay at that level."**

—The Millionaire Wholesaler

Click, Clack, and Your MQ

It was a simple enough errand.

That turned into a big aha moment.

The Mrs. and I were in route to Target and jumped into my fine ride (read: 2006 Honda pickup truck).

As I turned the key, the radio started playing the opening credits of one of my favorite NPR shows.

"Hello and welcome to Car Talk, with us Click and Clack, the Tappet Brothers."

The Mrs.: "Why are you listening to this—you don't even like car stuff."

Me: "True, but I do like them."

For those unfamiliar, here is the log line from their show: "America's funniest auto mechanics take calls from weary car owners all over the country and crack wise while they diagnose Dodges and dismiss Diahatsus."

And crack wise they did—for over thirty-five years.

They were able to interject the highest level of memorability into a subject that, for me, normally evokes a yawn (apologies to all car nuts).

Which, for a wholesaler, translates into being able to take topics that are the most mundane, events that are the most common, and interactions that are otherwise not the least bit noteworthy and turning them into catalysts to your MQ—Memorability Quotient®.

So what's your MQ?

Becoming an Automatic Wholesaler

Harvard Agency circa 1982.

A small executive-search firm in Los Angeles.

As we competed against larger firms, our goal was simply to get in the game.

To be considered in the same thought as the "big" players in the Los Angeles financial-services staffing community.

By 1992 the concept took on a larger stage: wholesaling eight states for OppenheimerFunds.

Our goal was simple—we wanted to become an Automatic.

We didn't want an advisor in the midst of a product decision to finalize her decision without speaking to us.

Because we knew if we were in the hunt, there was a high likelihood we would win the business.

It's similar to looking for a reliable car; you most likely will not buy until you test-drive a Honda.

Want a five-star hotel experience? You'll price Ritz Carlton as part of your investigation.

Honda, Ritz Carlton, and you achieve Automatic status through the following:

1. Relentless execution: There are no secret potions, no shortcuts, and a ton of sweat equity.

2. Stellar reputation: Everything, every day, is mindful of, and accretive to, your reputation and how you are perceived in the field.

3. Diligent development of a fan base: "Automatics" have fans, advocates, supporters, promoters, and believers.

How Automatic are you in the eyes of your clients and prospects?

———

"As you get more experienced, you become a reliable source."

—*The Millionaire Wholesaler*

Do Your Advisors Feel FOMO?

Call them VCs or angel investors.

They're folks who listen to endless pitches from wide-eyed, eternally hopeful entrepreneurs who think they have the next billion-dollar valuation.

In the pitch, angels need to feel the conviction of the entrepreneur's ideas.

They have to understand the new company's unfair advantage.

And when the entrepreneur is pitching well, they will instill FOMO—Fear of Missing Out.

Not too different from your role as a wholesaler.

With the advisor being your angel.

Do you deliver your product presentations and sales ideas with conviction?

Can you articulate or demonstrate the unfair advantage of both you and your firm?

And when, if you do manage to present with conviction and present the unfair advantage, is there any believable FOMO that you can display?

They are the technology hopefuls.

You are the hopeful wholesaler.

You share the same objective.

To get funded.

Your First Twenty-One Days

How many days does it take to form a habit?

Depends on who you ask.

A generally accepted and scientifically proven false time frame is twenty-one days.

Emanating out of a quote from a book called *Psycho-Cybernetics*; the twenty-one-day fallacy has been spread far and wide by some of the greatest self-improvement gurus.

More accurately, changing your wholesaling habits is a process.

One that can take months.

And along the way you're going to stumble.

Which, because you're a high-performance person, also means you'll unfairly kick yourself for that stumble.

So here's the deal: your Career Year starts today.

And during the next twenty-one business days, your job is to solidify your plan, clarify your process, and begin the implementation of your Career Year journey.

While recognizing and accepting that your road to success will be filled with potholes along the way.

Because it will be your process, tightly bolted in, that becomes the ultimate determinant of success.

"Discipline is the bridge between goals and accomplishment." —Jim Rohn

It's a Black-Brick Doorstop?

It was the dawn of a new decade.

The 1990s to be exact.

And the firm was moving full speed ahead with deploying technology—which, in 1993, sounded damn scary.

Arriving home after a week's worth of travel, my wife introduced me to a box the size of a miniature refrigerator.

Not at all excitedly, I unwrapped the contents and stared blankly at my new black brick.

An IBM ThinkPad that was made for a wholesaler on the go, as it weighted a mere 5.9 pounds.

Plus, the accompanying computer bag made for a great counterweight, opposite by garment bag slung over my other shoulder.

But lest I give you the wrong impression, that 5.9 lb. doorstop collected more dust than your great-aunt Hattie's attic.

Fast-forward to 2015, and we still have wholesalers who pronounce themselves as "old school."

But the great wholesaler knows that while the "old school" kids are searching for a pay phone with their pocket full of quarters, you are running technological and productivity laps around them.

What's your commitment to up your technology, organization, and productivity game in 2015?

———

"You need to be up on what's new, what's current and what's relevant."
—*The Millionaire Wholesaler*

A Wholesaler's Self-Deception

Cheese.

Wine.

A voracious midlife sweet tooth.

Add these all together and they equal the ten pounds that have mysteriously landed on my body in the past twenty months.

Though, if I stand just the right way, it's not so noticeable.

Plus I did work out yesterday, which means apple pie today is fine.

Are you as self-deceptive as I am?

Do you rationalize a marginal production month, when in your heart you know you've put in a half-assed effort?

Have you told yourself that you have no time for vacation, family events, or self-reflection because you're working so hard?

Do you believe that the way you did business five years ago will serve you five years from now?

The great news about what we do is that, day to day, no one is watching over our shoulder.

The bad news is we may not always tell ourselves the truth when we look in the rearview mirror.

"If it is necessary sometimes to lie to others, it is always despicable to lie to oneself." —W. Somerset Maugham

We Shoulda Stopped in Boonville

Population 894.

That's what the sign read as we rolled into Mendocino, California.

It's a beautiful blip on the map about a three-and-a-half-hour drive north of San Francisco.

Which means you'll need a full tank of gas to get there.

Which, in San Francisco, is around $2.40 per gallon.

And if you are running low on fuel on Highway 128, you'd better stop in Boonville.

Because you most assuredly don't want to get gas in Mendocino.

You see there are but two gas pumps in town, both at the same station.

Where the price per gallon is $5.45 [no, not a typo, $5.45].

It's as classic a case of supply and demand as you'll ever see—for a product that is the very definition of commoditized.

Which made me think of wholesalers and their often-heard refrain that their products, and even they, are commoditized.

Maybe, but what's your supply of insight, innovation, intellect, and ingenuity, to name a few?

Great wholesalers know that these attributes are always in demand—and often at a premium.

That Time I Outsourced Genuineness

It sure seemed like a great idea.

After all, I thought writing thank-you cards to advisors was a bit of a menial task.

So in year two of my wholesaling career, I decided to employ an assistant to write the cards.

And who better than Stacy, a sixteen-year-old whose brother was the manager of the local video store?

As I carefully explained the work that I did and who the audience for the cards would be, she looked like she was following along nicely.

I explained that the cards needed to look like they came from me, and so she needed to be mindful of the extra swirliness that accompanies most teenage girls' penmanship.

On Monday she was outfitted with a stack of thank-you cards, envelopes, and boilerplate language designed to express my appreciation for the advisor taking my meeting.

On Friday she returned to my office to proudly display her work.

Apparently my diligent explanations and careful instructions didn't quite land.

This was evidenced by the cute little circles dotting the i's and vertigo-inducing swoops of her letters.

Lesson learned.

Some things are just really difficult to outsource.

One for the Underdogs

Maybe you don't work for an eleven-hundred-pound gorilla of distribution.

Perhaps, like so many wholesalers, you have a massive multistate territory with more advisors than you can shake a stick at.

You are the dictionary definition of road warrior, as someone who lives in airports, hotels, and rental cars (versus local drivable regions).

The balancing act that you have to perform vis-à-vis work, spouse, friends, kids, and so forth is pure Cirque du Soleil in its execution.

You are your own internal, admin, and scheduler.

Frequently doing it all with a minimum of coaching, training, and motivation being delivered from your home office.

Sometimes, in the broad expanses of quiet and alone time that you have, you may question what you do.

So this one's for you.

For every mile.

For every night.

For every appointment.

And in honor of the Oscar season that is upon us:

"Sometimes it is the people no one imagines anything of who do the things that no one can imagine." —Joan Clarke, *The Imitation Game*

The Noise Between Your Ears

He hasn't flown in years.

The event that ruined his ability to fly took place six years ago, he explained.

He was on a cross-country flight and experienced, "the worst turbulence I could possibly imagine. I was certain that the plane was going to fall out of the sky," he said.

When he got to his East Coast destination, he was traumatized.

For three days he checked the Weather Channel looking for clear skies to make the flight home.

Ultimately, he was so paralyzed that he decided to take a three-day Greyhound bus ride back to his departure city, San Francisco.

He told me that he let the gremlins between his ears overtake his behavior.

Are you letting potentially irrational fears or limitations, the kind that germinate and fester between your ears, affect your ability to optimize your practice?

Sometimes we need to fight hard to control the gremlins between our ears—particularly those that limit our ability to reach new heights.

———

"Control the controllable."

—The Millionaire Wholesaler

Pick Up the Damn Phone

I'm a huge fan of email communication.

And you knew that—heck, we meet here every Sunday night.

Yet email can be our undoing too.

Recently, an app that I use every time I present live started throwing up a new error message.

Because of that error message, the functionality of the app that I rely on was stopped cold.

After clicking the Support link on their site, it was apparent that email was the only communication channel available.

Which may have been fine for the first couple of emails volleys.

Or the first day of problem diagnosis.

Or maybe, just maybe, if it was a small offshore company.

But after thirty-six hours; more than twenty emails; and a disheartening array of requests to uninstall, reinstall, hard restart, etc. from this Boston-based technology firm, I had reached my limit.

Fortunately I had the phone number of one of their senior executives.

He took the call, escalated the issue, and promised a senior tech would reach out.

Which he did.

Via email.

Sometimes we need to just pick up the damn phone!

———

"Not being afraid to call an advisor when things aren't going well is so important."
—*The Millionaire Wholesaler*

I'll Be Brief

One hundred fifty years ago.

That's how long it's been since a speech, one of the finest ever delivered, was spoken.

It commemorated the second inauguration of one of this nation's great leaders.

It spoke of a horrific war in which seven hundred thousand men died.

It asked that there be mutual forgiveness from both warring sides.

In his close, the words he spoke were so powerful that they now find a home carved into his memorial.

Abraham Lincoln's speech was a grand total of seven hundred words.

It lasted for a mere ten minutes.

As wholesalers we get paid to deliver highly effective and compelling messages.

We're reminded again that longer is not better.

Better is better.

There's No App for That

This week in New York City, I attended a business dinner in Lower Manhattan.

Of the many transportation alternatives to get there from Midtown, I opted for Uber.

Fire up the app, tap, watch the map for the driver's progress, and six minutes later we're off.

A clean, serviceable ride, if entirely impersonal.

Two days later, I needed to schedule a ride to JFK.

This time I called Mr. Luis, whom I've known for fifteen years, and had not seen in five.

Mr. Luis showed up early and greeted me with a hug.

In route to the airport, we caught up on his two sons, his four grandbabies, and his last vacation to visit his brothers in Spain.

We resumed the same comfortable conversation, as if I was in his car just last week.

It reminded me again of the importance of the relationships we build with the advisors and COIs whom we serve.

Yes, your advisors have access to more than enough product information and alternatives without you.

But when you do your advisor recon, demonstrate your value through your PVP—Peerless Value Proposition®, and work intentionally to reciprocally deepen the right relationships, your practice becomes technology proof.

And you become most memorable.

Your Return on Character

Is character directly correlated to a top wholesaler's performance?

What effect does character have on a leader's performance?

And can character be directly mapped to a company's return on assets?

Harvard Business Review published *Measuring the Return on Character*, which sought to look at how four CEO character traits effected company performance.

The article asked the big question, "Do highly principled leaders and their organizations perform especially well?"

The character traits measured, distilled from a far larger universe of possibilities, were integrity, responsibility, forgiveness, and compassion.

Recently I spoke to a large group of investment management senior leaders at a Money Management Institute conference.

The topic was "The Traits of The Millionaire Wholesaler."

Part of our work revealed that Millionaire Wholesalers take great pride, and attributed a part of their success, to character-related issues.

As you make your way through the week ahead, diligently focusing on the never-ending meetings, calls, and other assorted tasks, make time to think about your ROC—your return on character.

———

"Staying true to who you are, as an individual, is a key concept to success."

—*The Millionaire Wholesaler*

This Can't Possibly Be You

A good student of the business.

Like you, I try to stay informed about our niche of wholesaling, our economy, and our world.

And sometimes I read things that make my skin crawl and my head shake in disappointment.

Specifically, I came across an opinion piece in an industry publication that spoke to the need for wholesalers to be more discerning in selecting the advisors that they call on.

It was in the comments section that I read this, as written by an advisor:

This just happened 5 minutes ago.

I'm sitting in an appointment.

A wholesaler with a very large firm, breezes through the front door without an appointment.

Hands my assistant a piece of literature.

Made a tacky remark to her, while I had other clients out there who heard the remark, and then left.

No, this can't possibly be you.

Because you handle yourself with far more decorum and polish.

Or, because if you do drop in, you know how to do it properly.

———

"Be socially graceful and adapt to virtually any situation."
—*The Millionaire Wholesaler*

Your Cult Following

What do Lululemon, Harley-Davidson, and Apple have in common?

If you guessed that they are brands with a cult following, you'd have guessed right.

To be defined as a cult brand, The Cult Branding Company says that you are:

A product or service that is in a class of your own, as you have mastered the art of building lasting and meaningful relationships with your customers.

Cult brands have achieved a unique connection with customers and are able to create a culture that people want to be a part of.

Your brand, the one that stands proudly next to the brand of your firm, is as critical to your success as the product's five-year performance or the rate on its rider.

And, in a wholesaler's case, your brand is not the product or the service.

It is *you.*

"Wholesalers face the greatest danger
of trying to live by performance alone."

—*The Millionaire Wholesaler*

Just Waiting for a Crack

Presence in your absence.

It's the wholesaler's equivalent of advertising.

And when done consistently and correctly, all you need is the right crack in the competition's veneer.

For example:

For thirty years (yes, thirty), I've insured our autos with AAA.

Recently I received a notice that they couldn't quote a renewal because my roadside assistance had lapsed.

Seems that the automatic renewal failed and the notification of an expired credit card was never sent.

When I repurchased the roadside coverage, they started my relationship as if I were a new customer, with no acknowledgment of the thirty years.

More than simply annoyed, I just became curious—and for the first time shopped the renewal rate for auto that they quoted.

And now I am a GEICO customer, having saved 15 percent or more.

AAA showed the crack.

How well do you consistently and effectively execute your presence in your absence?

Shrimp Forks versus Swiss Army Knives

Utility is defined as

1. the state of being useful, profitable, or beneficial;

2. being able to perform several functions; and

3. functional rather than simply attractive.

In a recent conversation, as I was previewing a significant new product that may hit your wholesaling radar over the next year, we discussed how to make the product less like a shrimp fork and more like a Swiss Army knife.

Specifically I asked how the product would continue attract return users, because it was so useful, beneficial, and potentially profitable.

Because, unlike the lowly shrimp fork, that is only put on the far fringes of the formal table once or twice a year for special occasions, the Swiss Army knife can be used every day in so many ways.

Which got me thinking about your practice.

Yes, we assume that your product information is useful, profitable, or beneficial.

But, and here's the real test, are you able to perform several functions for your clients or prospects?

Or are you simply another pretty face (attractive) but not that functional?

Great wholesalers work on improving their utility and developing their PVP—Peerless Value Proposition®.

Never Stop

They were ubiquitous.

Old family memories were likely shot with an Instamatic camera, and the film was developed in their labs.

When you thought camera and/or film, you thought Kodak.

Or this company that in 1983 appeared on *Fortune*'s "Most Admired" list.

They founded enterprise technology that was synonymous with desktop calculators and word processing in the '60s and '70s.

Yet by 1985, with the rise of personal computers, Wang was on its way to extinction.

And for a period of time in the '70s and '80s, one Wall Street firm had an ad slogan that was hard-wired into the lexicon of the English language.

Though founded way back in 1904, the campaign "When E. F. Hutton talks, people listen" made the firm a household name.

But today, after scandals, fraud, and debt issues, the remains of original company are now buried in the archives of Citigroup.

Like these once-great companies, your practice constantly straddles the line.

The line between extraordinary success and the bottom decile of the firm's leader board.

Which is why you can't ever stop.

Learning.

Creating.

Evolving.

———

"Make sure you're never done learning."
—The Millionaire Wholesaler

Tripping Over Dollars to Pick Up Pennies

Big doins around here.

We're celebrating some milestone personal events, and along the way The Mrs. and I are traveling down memory lane.

While touring the first house we ever bought, the sellers were present for the showing.

As we entered the master bathroom, we noticed the big globs of caulking around the faucets.

When we inquired about the need for caulking, the seller said, "Oh, there's a leak, and my husband just wanted to pretty it up."

So rather than calling in a plumber to properly address the issue, which for one hundred dollars would have avoided the whole discussion, they chose to pretty it up.

And we chose to scrutinize the property even closer and made this a convenient price-negotiating point.

Similarly, there are likely areas of your practice that are covered over and/or held together with caulking.

Often, those minor shortcomings are simply masking larger deficiencies.

Deficiencies that, when revealed, will cost you business.

Where in your practice do you need to stop tripping over dollars to pick up pennies?

The Ocean of Rejection

You already know about the Sea of Sameness.

It's that body of water that will swallow you up, unless you learn how to distinguish yourself from your competition.

Recently I learned of another sales body of water.

The Ocean of Rejection.

According to Daniel Pink, this phrase was coined by Norman Hall who has, for the last forty years, sold Fuller Brushes door to door in San Francisco.

In those forty years, he learned the concept of Buoyancy— staying afloat in this ocean of rejection.

How?

One method is through Interrogative Self-Talk, a strategy used by the world's elite athletes.

Unlike simply stating positive affirmations such as, "I can do this," it's asking yourself questions.

"Can I do this?"

"How did I succeed the last time this situation presented itself?"

"What recent learnings do I have that I can apply to this client/prospect?"

Pink shares that this process of asking questions makes our mind work more efficiently and effectively and better prepares us for success.

How will you endure the Ocean of Rejection?

———

"When I hear the word 'no' it really just means not yet."
—*The Millionaire Wholesaler*

You're Not Lucky

She had a record sales month.

She said, "I just got lucky."

He got the elephant advisor to drop a huge ticket.

He chalked it up to right place, right time.

She made the annual wholesaler top-producer trip.

She said, "The stars just aligned I guess."

Luck is what happens when an unemployed pipe fitter from West Virginia wins $300 million in the Powerball lottery jackpot.

Right place and right time describes the hero who rescues a cat from a burning building that he happened to be walking by.

The stars (actually planets) align so infrequently as to be measured in decades, often centuries.

Great wholesalers work their butts off for every trade, every day.

Their processes are defined.

Their brands are distinct.

They create their success.

They don't get lucky.

———

"Treat everything very carefully, run it as a long-term business, and you get to have a long-term success."
—*The Millionaire Wholesaler*

The Introverted Extroverted Wholesaler

Raise your hand if, perhaps secretly, you are an introvert.

Yes, you're a wholesaler—a creature that, by alleged definition, is the consummate outgoing, life of the party, extrovert.

Truth be told, even though I am completely comfortable taking center stage in front of any size audience, I am an introvert.

Or am I, or are you?

At the University of Pennsylvania, Professor Adam Grant conducted research around the effectiveness of top sales professionals.

His findings revealed that the best performers were a mix of both introvert and extrovert.

They were ambiverts.

Turns out that ambiverts ask better questions.

Are better listeners.

And form better relationships.

—

**"Ask the right questions so that you can
get the advisor to open up."**
—The Millionaire Wholesaler

Death by Daily Sales

They come via voice mail.

They come via email.

There are parsed six ways from Sunday.

And, if you're not careful, they'll drive you mad.

They are the Daily Sales numbers.

For too many wholesalers, this readout sets the tone for how the rest of the day will go.

Great sales day and you're on top of the world.

Bad sales day and you're looking for a sword to reenact some ritual form of seppuku.

One of the single best pieces of advice I ever received about our world of sales was this:

You take care of the numbers and the numbers will take care of you.

So as the summer months descend on us and you are tempted to succumb to the myth of the summer doldrums, stay laser focused of your activity.

If you do you will be well taken care of.

———

"We cannot confuse busy work with productive activity."
—*The Millionaire Wholesaler*

Mayoral Meet and Greet

Years ago, while traveling in Manhattan, I had the opportunity to meet the mayor.

More specifically, the mayor of Tenth Avenue between 47th and 48th streets in Hell's Kitchen.

There, seated in front of Hell's Kitchen Pizza, was the proprietor, Russ.

Russ had to be the mayor because he knew everyone in the neighborhood.

Each person who passed his perch gave him a wave and a nod, honked their horn, or otherwise acknowledged his presence.

He demonstrated what it's like to stake your claim, even inside of a huge region—that little hamlet called Manhattan.

Russ ran a business that people wanted to personally connect with, in a town that has no shortage of dough, sauce, and cheese.

He was memorable by virtue of his personality, his presence, and his pie.

Whether you work in a major market, such as Metro New York, Los Angeles, and Chicago, or ply your craft in the Big Square states, are you the mayor of your territory?

Do you have command over your region in the way that Russ commanded Tenth Avenue between 47th and 48th?

Three-Step Wholesaler Cleanse

Caffeine withdrawals.

Seems that an old friend was experiencing them after going through a nine-day cleanse, which included four days of fasting.

Not one to undertake any regimen that involves removing Starbucks from my life, I started thinking about ways to cleanse my practice—and how you can cleanse yours.

Specifically, what three things can you do today that will make you more productive, feel less overwhelmed, and maybe, just maybe, take back some time in your life?

1. Revisit every tone, vibration, and ring from every app and device you own. Make the often-hard decision to simply turn off most of them.

Cleanse yourself of the noise and distraction.

2. Get the constant swirl of ideas out of your head and get them onto paper (app). Or as David Allen says, "Your head is for having ideas, not holding them."

Cleanse yourself of the mental clutter.

3. Your overwhelming list of things to do isn't ending, but you can manage how you feel about that list by focusing on the biggest or ugliest tasks first thing every day

and identifying the Big Three Things that will allow you to call the day a success.

Cleanse yourself of the "everything is urgent" mentality.

———

"You need strong time management skills."
—*The Millionaire Wholesaler*

A Hustler's Paradise

He was easy to spot, as soon as I exited the terminal.

There was something about his look that just screamed Los Angeles.

His mid-thirties, hope-to-be-leading-man image suggested that his town car driver gig was simply to help pay the bills while working for his big break.

Sure enough, about two minutes into the drive, the flood gates opened when I asked, "So are you an actor?"

Which, in Los Angeles, is akin to asking a sommelier if she drinks.

Peter rattled off the high concepts and anticipated financing of deals he was hoping to launch.

"I've done pretty good in the three years I've been here from the South Bronx," he said.

"This town is more open than folks think. The opportunity is here; you just need to work hard for it," he explained. "From the time I get out of bed until the time my head hits the pillow, I'm hustling, because this town is a hustler's paradise!"

Maybe wholesaling and acting aren't that different.

The great wholesaler is always on an audition, hoping to win a call back and land a starring role in an advisor's book of business.

Because regardless of where they ply their craft, great wholesalers know that they too live in a hustler's paradise.

———

"Go above and beyond, work harder than other wholesalers."
—*The Millionaire Wholesaler*

Until They Know How Much You Care

What do you call it when the stars align and you have a magical moment with a client or prospect?

Or, in this case, with a fellow wholesaler.

When I'm asked to work live with a team of wholesalers, one mission-critical topic is the ability to perform reconnaissance work on the advisor—before the wholesaler's cheeks hit the advisor's guest chair.

Because time and again, we see the power of touching the advisor's head and their heart.

The night before a recent wholesaler meeting, I learned, via my online research, that one of the participants started a nonprofit with his wife specifically to address the impact of, and recovery from, concussions in student athletes.

Their motivation was a heartening story with a happy ending that they endured with their son.

When I approached the wholesaler in the meeting room with our patented setup and delivery of what I learned, it was crystal clear to the whole room that I had touched a powerful nerve.

Powerful enough for the wholesaler to comment to me afterward that he appreciated that moment.

Your ability to do your advisor homework and deliver those findings in the appropriate way will have a meaningful impact on the success of your meetings.

And further elevate you out of the Sea of Sameness.

Are you making time to do your advisor recon?

———

"No one cares what you're saying until they know that you care."
—The Millionaire Wholesaler

No Go, We're Status Quo

He became my obsession.

For years I called on Dan, determined to find the angle that would convert him from dabbler to top producer.

But I now know his cards were mentally stacked against me—and they frequently are for your top prospects too.

How many times have you heard a prospect explain that they are unmotivated to make a change?

Enter the Status Quo Bias.

How powerful a force is this bias?

Consider the small German town that was asked to relocate to facilitate a mining project.

The government was prepared to move the entire town's population and infrastructure to a nearby valley—and custom-build the town to the preferences of the residents.

So what did they choose?

An exact replica of the old town, complete with a Byzantine network of nonsensical roads dating back hundreds of years.

So how do you overcome status quo bias in advisors?

One way is to properly probe, diagnose a need, and then present one option.

Note the word "one."

A Harvard study on the topic found that "the more options that were included in the choice set, the stronger the relative bias for the status quo."

"To do nothing is within the power of all men." —Samuel Johnson.

Great wholesalers know that unleashing the entire contents of their product bag of tricks exacerbates the status quo.

Is It the Thought That Counts?

We forgive the little things.

It's better human nature.

Your significant other buys you a gift that's the wrong size or color, and you remark, "It's the thought that counts."

And in an interpersonal relationship that may be true.

But in business it's not.

For example, The Mrs. and I recently celebrated our twenty-fifth anniversary at a resort that was billed as super swanky.

Always a thoughtful touch, the manager sent a bottle of champagne and a card to the room to acknowledge the event.

It was in this moment that the resort could choose to dazzle or fizzle out.

Sadly it was the latter.

Unfortunately when an employee knocks at the door and hands you a warm bottle of bubbly (no ice, no bucket), two glasses, and a card, a maneuver that may require a third hand, it makes you question when the swank came out of swanky.

Not unlike the commoditization of wholesaling, there is no shortage of higher-end hotels and resorts that are all clamoring to earn your business.

In a world where a product or service becomes indistinguishable from others, laser-focused attention to detail can be the difference between raving fans and one-hit wonders.

Your Picture of Success

What does success look like to you?

Is it measured in dollars and cents?

Or is it defined by examining the leader board at your firm?

What goals stand before you in the next 365 days?

How will you ensure that the year ahead will be your year?

The one in which you break through.

The one in which you conquer.

The one in which your picture of success is in clear, full, bright, living color.

The good news: the wholesaling clock can start anew starting today.

The bad news: only a small percentage of folks will edit their picture, even after reading this far.

The canvas is blank.

Go make the rest of your career a beautiful picture of success.

_____

"Short memory, thick skin—two essential ingredients for long term wholesaling success."
—*The Millionaire Wholesaler*

We are so fortunate to work in an industry that affords us so much opportunity. At Wholesaler Masterminds, we constantly seek out both the largest-scale issues and the most nuanced subtleties that will give you the wholesaling edge. If we can help you in moving from good wholesaler to great wholesaler, please send us an email at wholesalermasterminds@gmail.com.

To sign up for the Wholesaler Masterminds®
Sunday Night Email
or for the latest articles, podcasts,
and videos, be sure to visit
us at

Wholesaler Masterminds®
WHERE GOOD WHOLESALERS BECOME GREAT WHOLESALERS

www.wholesalermasterminds.com

About the Author

Rob Shore has over thirty-five years of experience in financial services, with twenty-five of those years spent in distribution. His proven background in corporate America has provided him with a reputation as a leader who has been recognized for innovation, results, creativity, and, most importantly, extraordinary sales success.

Rob was part of the "new wave" of brokers in banks circa 1987, and he cut his wholesaling teeth at Oppenheimer-Funds, where he helped build Oppenheimer's early entry into bank distribution as one of the channel's founding wholesalers—and where he maintained the number-one wholesaling rank for four consecutive years.

Later, as president of Allstate Distributors, LLC, Rob led the activities of cross-channel product distribution and marketing that produced over $30 billion in top-line sales and achieved 30 percent annual compounded sales growth.

Today he is the CEO of shorespeak, L.L.C., which publishes WholesalerMasterminds.com, the de facto online destination for financial services wholesaling professionals and the *Wholesaler Masterminds Radio* podcast. Rob was the publisher and editor-in-chief at *I Carry The Bag* magazine, the official magazine of wholesaling, and authored the predecessor to this book, *Brotherhood of the Bag: A Wholesaler's Handbook.*

He is a frequent speaker at national sales conferences and divisional meetings and devotes his extensive private coaching practice to two groups: wholesalers and their leaders.

He lives with his wife and a gaggle of small domestic animals in the California wine country.